YOU CAN

A COLLECTION OF BRIEF TALKS ON THE MOST IMPORTANT TOPIC IN THE WORLD — YOUR SUCCESS

GEORGE MATTHEW ADAMS

Srishti
PUBLISHERS & DISTRIBUTORS

Srishti Publishers & Distributors
A unit of AJR Publishing LLP
212A, Peacock Lane
Shahpur Jat, New Delhi – 110 049

editorial@srishtipublishers.com

First published by
Srishti Publishers & Distributors in 2024

10 9 8 7 6 5 4

Printed and bound in India

You Can

YOU CAN make of yourself anything the germ of which lives within you. But to realize your full possibilities — to Dominate and Achieve — you must have High Aims, Ideals and Ambitions — all linked to an Iron Will. You yourself determine the height to which you shall Climb. Have you the Summit in view? All right — Then Start for it.

YOU CAN take command of yourself at any moment you desire to do so. You can make yourself a towering figure in the work of the world. No one owns you.

One hundred per cent of the Stock in your personal Corporation belongs to you. The little People of Destruction that whine at your door, whine at the door of every forceful man. You can make them mere Pygmies in their Power over your Future. Are you doing this Now? Well — Then Keep it up!

YOU CAN get Smiles and Cheer and Continued Youth — simply by sticking to your own craft and running your own pilot wheel with "Your Best" as the Place of Port. Results will take care of themselves. Never mind the Sneers, the Criticisms, the Misjudgments of others. Time will fade them all away from you if your Accumulated Strength of Character has taught you how to Wait. Today is Yesterday's plans put into action. Tomorrow begins Today. Your Worth to yourself and the World is measured by what you contribute each day in Usefulness. Success is the Sum of the Days.

Then Do Today.

YOU CAN make Success sure by Work, Sacrifice, Enthusiasm, Unselfishness and Self-control. You are the Master of your own Destiny. Take personal command of yourself Today.

YOU CAN!

50-50

NO man in all this world ever rightfully Gets more than he Gives. And if he does he is just a plain Thief — a discredit first to Himself, then to everybody else. The Equal Division is always the Just

Division — half to you and half to him. In other words, on the basis — 50-50.

Be glad to Give as much as you Take.

You who are an Employee, are you Sure you are giving in Service as much as you are taking in Money,

Experience, Inspiration and Training from your Employer? Right now, take invoice. Do the results look

like — 50-50? If not, start this plan into action —

Be glad to Give as much as you Take.

This plan of 50-50 — rightly interpreted, means death to Whiners, to the Disgruntled, and to the Assassinators of Success. They can't live in the atmosphere of it. The Air is too Invigorating.

Be glad to Give as much as you Take.

Every dispute in this World is traceable to the lack of the 50-50 principle. The broken-up Homes, the disintegrated Businesses, the abandoned Friendships, the wasteful Armies of the World. There is need of this principle in every phase of Life. But never will it become a rule of every-day Action until YOU, in your place, begin to apply — 50-50.

Be glad to Give as much as you Take.

Silence

YES, Silence is many times Golden. You know If that. But try to realize it more strongly. For the Silent Man is usually the Thinking Man and the Silent Worker is the Get-Things-Done Worker. But best of all, Silence as a rule of daily life Conduct makes you Big and Powerful.

Don't talk Back.

The World's great Doers have all been Men and Women of few words — Napoleon, Cromwell, Washington, Grant, Lincoln, Marshall Field — Edison. These men didn't have time for disputes, wrangles — revenges.

Don't talk Back.

The World is coming to the Idea of Silence — fewer Words, more Deed-doing. It is the big Law of Nature. It is becoming the great Law of Business. For silence can't be answered. There is nothing to answer.

Don't talk Back.

Look around you. You admire the Silent people — those who mind their own business and Build. You know the names of the Useful men of your town. You can't waste their time — you can't get them "mad." You can't steal anything from them. Their Silence is their Wealth and every time they walk along the streets they speak volumes. Add another motto to those you may already have. Make it this — Silence.

Don't talk Back.

Health

FEW people wear out before their time. Mostly they Rust out, Worry out, Run out — Spill out. A Machine must have care and its different parts must be adjusted properly. No Machine has ever approached the Human Machine. When it is right, it is in Health.

Make Confidants of Air and Exercise.

No great Battle was ever won with antiquated Artillery. Nor is it possible for Men or Women to give the best that is in them, aided by weak, ill cared for, abused Bodies. For Health puts on the alert every quality of Soul and makes the Brain and Heart and Nerve stations work in even unison, throbbing out big things in Deeds.

Make Confidants of Air and Exercise.

Pure Air, wholesome Exercise, a few good "Hobbies" put an edge to a human being that all the Pills in creation can't equal. In addition, by touching up your Pace with plenty of 22-Karat Smiles, you have briefly a Home Remedy for Health of great power and very practicable.

Make Confidants of Air and Exercise.

You have time to eat, you have time to make money, you have time to take to your bed when abuse brings on aches — you will have to take time to die. It is good sense, then, to take time to get Health.

Make Confidants of Air and Exercise.

Everybody is quickened and inspired by the vibrating Health and warm Magnetism that is felt instantly from the Healthy man. He is the man who does things. He is the man who is a Success. He is the fellow who has time to take on Air and Exercise and grasp Health.

Also he is the one who accomplishes twice the work of the weakling and has the MOST time.

Make Confidants of Air and Exercise.

If you aspire for large jobs, of necessity you must aspire for — and get — a vigorous Body, filled to the brim with Health. Half of Health is in the Mind. The rest is in getting into the Air and giving every Muscle of the body and every organ a good daily stirring tip with use and Exercise. Let this thought radiate from your face and bearing toward every man, woman, or child that you meet: "I am a Happy, Healthy Human Being!"

Make Confidants of Air and Exercise.

Character

CHARACTER is the sum total, worth while, of what a man has after he has won all and the sole thing he has left after he has lost all.

Character is Power.

J. Pierpont Morgan, the greatest single power in Finance in all the world, at the time of his death, once stated under oath, that "Character is the only gauge of a man, or the only rule by which he can be gauged in business, and that physical assets are therefore of secondary importance."

Character is Power.

The walls of Character that a man builds will withstand the most merciless assaults that any man can direct at them. A man's or a woman's good Character is absolutely unassailable. Reputation may be besmirched — but not Character. For Reputation is what people may say a man is, but Character is what he really is.

Character is Power.

Character is greater than talent, genius, fame, money, friends — there is nothing to compare with it. A man may have all these and yet remain comparatively useless — be unhappy — and die a bankrupt in Soul. But — Character pays out endless Dividends, molds a man into a mighty Deed-doer, and builds for him a deathless Name.

Character is Power.

Character is Power in Business, in the Home, on the Street —

everywhere. And it's free for the asking to the man willing to be kind, honest, square, broad, generous, loyal, fearless — Big! Stamp your Character deeper on people Today and make it rule your work. Let it lead you on. But fight every hour to make it stronger.

for —

Character is Power.

Mistakes

STUDY your Mistakes.

There are two kinds of Mistakes. Those that happen from ordinary human mis-thinking and those that come from carelessness and petty un-thinking.

Study your Mistakes.

No one ever gets too big to make Mistakes. The secret is that the big man is greater than his Mistakes, because he rises right out of them and passes beyond them.

After one of Henry Ward Beecher's sermons in Plymouth Church, Brooklyn, a young man came up to him and said: "Mr. Beecher, did you know that you made a grammatical error in your sermon this morning?"

"A grammatical error," answered Beecher, "I'll bet my hat that I made forty of them."

Half of the power of the forceful man springs out of his Mistakes of one sort or another. They help to keep him human?

Study your Mistakes.

But the Mistakes that tear away the power of a man, weaken him, and make him flabby, are the stupid, the reckless Mistakes. The Clerk who forgets, the Stenographer that doesn't care, the Worker who neglects — these are the ones whose life blood and vitality is sapped and sucked away into failure.

Study your Mistakes.

One of the great things of each day for you is to do your best — unmindful of Mistakes. But after your work is done and you realize your blunders, don't shirk, don't whine, don't despond, but —

Study your Mistakes.

Then profit from them — and go ahead!

Ruts

ONE of the important lessons of this life is to learn to keep out of Ruts. Everyone is bound to strike them at times. But they should be gotten out of — immediately. For to stay in a Rut is to stick still — and stagnate, while others pass you and forget you.

Keep your eyes Open and your Mind Awake.

Watch out for the Imitation Rut — the Rut that takes you away from your own Work and your own Ideas and makes a Duplicate out of you instead of an Original. Creators stand in a class by themselves. Pay tribute to the Head on your own shoulders. Get the habit of Initiation.

Keep your Eyes Open and your Mind Awake.

Think. Get together new Ideas. Welcome them. Read. Profit from the Minds of past ages. Compare them with the advancing Thought and Experiences of your own age. Delve into the Mysteries. Seek out the Truths they hold. Learn SOMETHING new each day — and you will be ready armed against getting into Ruts.

Keep your Eyes Open and your Mind Awake,

Vary your Work each day as greatly as possible. Think out new ways of doing old Tasks. The Brain acts spryest when it is most interested. Love your Work. If you don't, find Work that you do.

Keep your Eyes Open and your Mind Awake.

And be kind to your own human Machine. Give it Rest. Occasionally dip away into new Surroundings, see new Faces, and meet new Scenes. Find delight among those who Do and Dare Lock arms with the

Smilers — pass by the Frowners. Now, read this little talk over again — resolving that you will from this time on stay out of the Rut business.

Together

FOR the sake of this little Talk, let us suppose that the one word Together is derived from the three words – TO GET THERE. It is quite possible, anyway. For when people get themselves Together, or you collect all your individual forces Together, the thing aimed at usually happens.

TO GET THERE is to get Together.

Analyze a Human Failure. Here is what you learn. He is all apart — all unhitched. His Brain is without organization. Most of his fine sensibilities are stunned or dead. His Will isn't Landlord any more. It's just a Boarder — and half starved at that. His original force of Executives and assistants — once alert and healthy and willing — have all gone out into the yard to Doze. Confusion and Ruin is everywhere. Chaos reigns. What is the Remedy? This —

TO GET THERE is to get Together.

It's marvelous the change that comes about when a man gets Together all his Forces and centers them upon the doing of ONE thing at a time. The Together idea is the progressive idea. "Where there is a Will, there is a Way." But the Will is of no use without the Plan back of the Will. Plan, Will — Way. All Together and things are accomplished.

TO GET THERE is to get Together.

When you begin to Divide your interests or to Distribute your forces, you begin to lose your Grip. As you draw all your Forces Together, you increase your Power. Big things are done on the Together plan.

Bird shot will kill small game but it takes the single
Rifle balls to bring down the big game.
TO GET THERE is to get Together.

Weigh and consider this thought as you face your work each day. Give it an honor place as a working rule. Get Together. Then stick Together.

Win

THE very first commandment in the decalogue of Winning is to —

Keep your Chin up!

Get busy at the first job that you run into or that runs into you. Tackle it "on all fours," if necessary. Center your whole enthusiasm in it. Study its every detail. Drive your very Heart interest into it. But don't forget to —

Keep your Chin up.

People who look down never get much of an idea of the sky where the Stars are set. And the fellow who doesn't hitch at least one or two of his wagons to a Star never gets very high up. Get your eyes off the ground. Look ahead.

Keep your Chin up.

For, after all, Winning is a thing within — then out. No other man will or can Win for you. No other man in all the world, no matter how exalted, has the ability and power that is concentrated in you, waiting for some match of Action to touch it off. Also, your Success can be as the Success of no other man. But you alone must find the Thing and DO the Work. It's great fun, too, if you —

Keep your Chin up.

It is easier to Win than to Fail. Everybody sides with the Winner. But the Failure walks alone.

Keep your Chin up.

Remembering that to Win is to do your work well — today. The thing delayed or put off is the thing undone. Start right now. Straighten your shoulders. Set your eyes ahead. Clench your fist — close your jaw, and —

Keep your Chin up.

And you will WIN!

Time

"The reason I beat the Austrians is, they didn't know the value, of five minutes." — Napoleon,

LEARN to use your Time.

For if you don't it passes on, never to return —

coldly mindless of your sorrow and your regret.

As steadily, silently and smoothly as does this aged Earth move in its path, so does Time move on. It never stops to tie its shoestrings. It never waits.

Time is Effort, harnessed and worked to a full day's portion.

Time has no Business, boasts no monied Millions, hires no fast-legged Errand Boys, houses no Clerks, thinks no Problems, rules no States. Time IS Business, Money, the Errand Boy, the Clerk, the Problem, the State!

Time is but the man in the job put to action and to work.

And Time used to profit Today will accumulate Power for you Tomorrow just as sure as Time goes on. Meditate not on Trifles. Attempt big things. Remembering that —

This day will never dawn again!

And yet, mighty as Time is, priceless in comparison to all else in the world, Time is the freest thing in existence. Perhaps that is why so many fail to grasp it with earnestness and with enthusiasm? Perhaps that is why so few realize its presence and let it pass on?

Think! No matter what your work today, if it is worth while at all — Time to plan it out, Time to do it well, and Time to finish it, is your day's greatest gift and your greatest job.

Learn to use your Time.

Success

IN Success, defeat is but an incident. Obstacles, stumbling blocks, disappointment in ideals — these things weave into and form the Raiment to Success. For Success is a series of failures — put to flight.

Learn to walk past Failure.

A few years ago, a young man stood behind a New England counter as a Clerk. Quiet, honest, faithful yet a Failure in the eyes of his Employer, who one day drew aside the father of the boy and advised that the son be taken back to the farm for he never would become a Merchant. Today if you will but walk down State Street, Chicago, you will behold this young man's monument — a tribute to the failures, disappointments and iron persistence of Marshall Field, who died the greatest Merchant in the World.

Learn to walk past Failure.

But Success isn't measured in tangible assets. Lincoln left next to nothing in money standards. His Success, though, is the marvel and inspiration of the Ages.

Learn to walk past Failure.

Success is largely a matter of personal Viewpoint.

It is impossible for you to fail permanently if you determine to Succeed. Let each new day of your life then, take invoice of its own self. Let it chalk up the Failures with the Successes — let it mark plainly the Record. But inside of your own consciousness let nothing take from the image of your mind, the Knowledge that real Success consists wholly in sacrificing temporarily in repeated failures that you may win permanently in worth while Deeds done.

Learn to walk past Failure.

Dare

IMMORTALITY is but a simple matter of Decision — a Decision to Dare.

Initiate — Dare.

All the world loves the man who isn't afraid to Dare — a man willing to start something without first waiting a week to figure out the cost. It always takes Courage — Sometimes courage mixed with "blood and iron." But the man ready to Dare is the creator of great Events?

Initiate — Dare.

Better make mistakes — better blunder along making some healthy headway, than to fear Failure or grow timid and vacillating and flabby in the legs. Become a man of Daring and Doing and the Powers that are so latent in every human will rise to aid you and push you on.

Initiate — Dare.

You will never be Anything, unless you Dare Something.

Initiate — Dare.

Dare to attempt new things. Dare to try out new Jobs. Dare to go ahead, kicking aside Precedent if necessary, and you will have no time to shovel out of your pain wrecked Hopes and dead Dreams. Dare to be a better man at your present task than the man who went before you. Dare to be a bigger man than the man above you. Be. But, if you are, you will first have to —

Initiate — Dare.

Backbone

THERE are two kinds of Backbones — the one with the Back and no Bone and the one with both Back and Bone! Backbone! what great things have been put across in your name!

Stiffen your Backbone.

It is a great thing to have a big Brain, a fertile Imagination, grand Ideals, but the man with these, bereft of a good Backbone is sure to serve no useful end.

Stiffen your Backbone.

There is a little vine that starts at the base of the great trees. Then it climbs and twines about until it squeezes and saps away unto death the tree around which it clings. It has not a Backbone — no vital individual strength of its own, so it seeks out to tear down and kill where there is strength, power and life. That is what Backbone-less people do.

Stiffen your Backbone.

Use it to stand alone with. Use it to bolster up your own individual resources. Use it to strengthen weaker Backbones than your own. Use it for the working out of your entire Character. Then Deeds Done, will gather about you in Battalions, and Opportunity will stand around anxious to introduce you to her friends.

Stiffen your Backbone.

Use your Backbone at your job today — you who clerk, you whose fingers pound the type keys, you whose brains formulate plans, distribute details and master problems. For the temple of Success is upheld by the strong arms of men and women who have Backbone and use it.

Pay

EMERSON says that "the strongest man on earth is the man who stands most alone." Owe money — be in Debt — and you stand by the props that the sweat of other men's brows and the gray of other men's brains have earned and bought. You don't stand alone. You play false to your own strength.

Abhor Debt. Pay.

Debt means to owe — somebody else. It means that you give up what might be yours. It means that you offer a part of yourself for sale for a definite sum. When you owe money, you make yourself a slave. The other fellow holds you fast in literal bondage.

Abhor Debt. Pay.

Better live happy away from glamor, smooth words, hand-clapping, and selfish gratification than Dog to some Master whose whistle you are bound to respect.

Abhor Debt. Pay.

The quickest way to kill a Friend (the most valuable possession on Earth) is to ask him to lend you money. If he is a real Friend he will refuse. If you are a real Man you will learn a lesson and thank him. The man who makes it a rule to live within his means soon creates means to live out of it. There is but one safe, sound, sensible rule in money affairs and that is to /pay as you

go — or don't go.

Abhor Debt. Pay.

Start today to Pay up. Will yourself to do it. Catch fire and enthusiasm from the freedom and power that follow in the way of the man who owes not a dollar to any man.

Abhor Debt. Pay.

Count

IF there IS any pure Luck in the world or if it ever really does figure in the summing up of things, here's when it figures biggest — on the day that you find your Life Work — and glory in it. Lucky you are, then — for you — Count. The world must have you.

Be Somebody in the Crowd — Count.

No man ever Counts until he assumes Responsibility. Responsibility demands the work of the Brain and Heart. These two, working together, breed Ideas. Then Results begin to show. And Results make you Count.

Be Somebody in the Crowd — Count.

People who are Useful always Count. So if you want to Count — if you want to be singled out and justly praised, think of the most useful service possible for you to render. Then get busy in doing it. You at your job, doing it as best you can, are sure to Count.

Be Somebody in the Crowd — Count.

Nothing stirs and inspires more than to have it said that you are Somebody and that — you Count — that you are a Creator, a Builder, a Producer. Anyone is justified in congratulating himself if he does things — if he really Counts.

Be Somebody in the Crowd — Count.

But don't be so foolish as to be completely satisfied

with the results of any work. Growth comes in a large

measure by Comparison. When you do your work better Today than Yesterday, you realize your genuine Capacity and know that there is no actual Perfection except the Perfection of doing better Today than Yesterday. Strive for this and you need to have no concern as to whether or not you will Count. You will.

Why

BEFORE you do a thing — ask Why? A great deal of the Lost Motion of the world results from Head-long Action — going into a task without Cause — without some definite Purpose — without first finding out — Why.

Before you do a thing — ask Why?

Let Why lead you on and cave you Power. Simply answer with promptness its Silent questionings. Give unto Why a substantial reason for the fiber that is within you.

Before you do a thing — ask Why?

Ask yourself: "Why should I do this thing? Why should I refuse to do it?" Put your actions to the Why test. Think of the wealth of happiness that the habitual use of Why can bring you!

Before you do a thing — ask Why?

Make Why very personal. "Why do I squander so much Time? Why do I appreciate so little the chance to live? Why do I use so small a fraction of my Brain Ability? Why do I not make more Friends? Why do I worry about things that Never Happen? Why do I scold when I should Cheer?" Why?

Before you do a thing — ask Why?

Keep Why busy about your House. And at the Night-fall of each day gather into convention the Whys of each Thought and Act.

Before you do a thing — ask Why?

Eliminate the regretful Why. Put yourself on the Stand hourly. Ask and Answer with fortitude and freedom — unafraid of Right conscientiously performed.

Frankness

FRANKNESS is the art of saying things you honestly think exactly as you think them. To be Frank is to be naturally straightforward.
Look the other fellow in the Eye.

Just as a straight line is the shortest distance between two points, so is Frankness the only right course between all people. Because nothing is wasted. The Frank man is the only man worthy of trust.
Look the other fellow in the Eye.

Frankness between Employer and Employee, Frankness between a Man and a Woman, Frankness between yourself and the one who disagrees with you, is the only sensible way.
Look the other fellow in the Eye.

The beginning of mutual respect is trust. No satisfactory result in anything was ever achieved without Frankness.
Look the other fellow in the Eye.

Never think that Frankness is Impudence, nor crude Opinion. It is the face to face openness of Mind and Heart that challenges immediate acceptance of what you have to say as the uncoated Truth.
Look the other fellow in the Eye.

Today, don't hedge. Stand squarely on your own legs. Be Frank. And you will marvel at the ease with which other people will understand and respect you. Frankness, a very precious possession, is possible to all — save one, the Coward? You — start to put Frankness into use.

Make it earn its board and lodging. Say out what you have to say — with Frankness.

Look the other fellow in the Eye.

Faces

THE most marvelous of all pieces of work, is the human Face. Strange that out of all the billions of Faces made since Time got to going, no two Faces have ever been exactly alike. Strange, too, that no one Face long remains the same!

Make Something of YOUR Face.

The Face is the Revelation of Character. As surely and positively as does the hand guided by the orders of the Brain clear wide wastes, build great cities, and cut into life-like figures from bare rocks the story of men's achievements, so does the Brain and Thought of a man carve and fashion daily the secret workings of his Ideals and Purposes into the Lines and Planes of his own Face.

Make Something of YOUR Face.

There is one thing a man cannot hide from — his own Face! Where the Man goes the Face must go. How tremendous the responsibility, then, of making your Face a good Companion, a faithful Servant, an active Force, an interesting Study — a Face worth remembering!

Make Something of YOUR Face.

The only way to make Something of your Face is to make Something of your Character.

A Face never lies. It may be a Comic Picture, a Comedy of Errors, a Shakespearean Tragedy, a chiseled piece of Power, or a wrecked god — but it is no lie. If you would know your Friend, study the history of his Face.

Make Something of YOUR Face.

No one could get a hearing if he wrote a whole library of malicious tales about Lincoln. His wonderful Face would contradict them all. To learn what manner of person a man is, study his Face. His Character is proclaimed there as Trumpet Tones. Pope said that the proper study of mankind was man. But the way to study a man is to study his Pace. Be not so foolish as to try to "hop bail" on your own Pace. You can't. Better start associating more with it. It is your largest asset, for no man can take it from you. Realize now, then, that the most important job for you each day is -

Make SOMETHING of your Face.

Responsibility

A great man by the name of Ansalus de Insulis — remember the name — once wrote these wonderful words: "Learn as if you were to live forever; live as if you were to die tomorrow."

Be Responsible, first, to Yourself.

Responsibility is one thing that all must face and that none can escape. It starts with the baby in the cradle. It never ends! For the Responsibility of a man goes on even after his work in the flesh is over. A man performs a great deed. It lives in printed pages and goes on in its influence as long as there is any life in the world at all.

Be Responsible, first, to Yourself.

Individual Responsibility! It's the thing that makes the Man. Without it there is no Man. Bear in mind, you who must realize Responsibility to your Employer, or to your Friend, or to your Home, — your first Responsibility is to Yourself. And if you are weak and false to yourself — if you wabble in doing the things that mean your very life and Success — you are already a Failure.

Be Responsible, first, to Yourself.

Then PEEL your Responsibility. No one is useless who believes that some things depend upon him alone. You who read this little preachment, take it to heart. Be unafraid of at least attempting larger things. Convince your own self that you have worth and can prove it — and the tasks of big moment will take care of you and lift you into importance and affluence — the gifts of having the courage to take Responsibility and shoulder it. But, remember to —

Be Responsible, first, to Yourself.

Happiness

HAPPINESS is Helpfulness bubbling over at the rim. Also, Happiness is getting in tune with the music of the Band of The-Out-of-Doors. There is no unhappiness in Nature.

Lend a Hand. Make Happiness a Habit.

The people who are Happy are the people who are Successful — not in money, merely, but in Contentment, realized Aims and completed Effort. To win — be Happy. To be Happy — do something worthwhile.

Lend a Hand. Make Happiness a Habit.

The fastest growing concern is the one with the most Happy helpers. Happiness produces health. Health plows up the field of native ability and makes ready the soil for the Happy Harvest.

Lend a Hand. Make Happiness a Habit.

Happiness cannot be bought. Being rated as of all things about the most Precious — it is at the same time free. It is for all. But there must be mustered the effort to take it. And after you have it, if you would keep it — give it away.

Lend a Hand. Make Happiness a Habit.

For Happiness boiled down is nothing more nor less than being well content with your progress by seeking better things all the time, being glad that you are alive, thanking God that you have a chance, believing that you have some things that nobody else in all the world has, and just resolving that you are going to make this world a marvelous place to stay in for a while. It's also having something that everyone else will want — and giving it to others.

Lend a hand. Make Happiness a Habit.

Service

TO SERVE is to find Something to do — and then do it. It matters not what this Something is, so long as it serves a Useful end.

Honor your Job.

The biggest man or woman who ever lived, was in no way, after all, greater than a Servant — in some way or other. The world is a world of Servants. You are a Servant. The one you Serve is a Servant.

Honor your Job.

Proportionately every man is as great as the greatest if he Serves to his fullest Capacity. To do this is to Grow. And Growth only comes to the people of Capacity. You who do your best today will do better tomorrow. To Service there is no limit.

Honor your Job.

No occupation is so dignified as Service of some kind. Nothing brings greater rewards in Happiness and Power. He climbs highest who helps another up.

Honor your Job.

The true fact in all this world is that the more you do for someone else, the more you boost your own game — the stronger your own individual influence and Character becomes. Suppose you try it out today and learn for yourself. Try it in your Home, at your Office, in your place of power or in the midst of the humblest circumstances. Be a real Servant. Serve. And be glad in doing it.

Honor your Job.

And by so doing become one of the factors in the stirring affairs of your time.

Imagination

IMAGINATION is the greatest asset that the world's Doers have ever had. Money, titles, estates — they are all cheap beside this marvelous gift. Imagination is the creator of them all in most instances.

Cultivate your Imagination.

You who read this — did you ever stop to consider that you would not be worth the free air you breathe were it not for the fact that you possess to some extent the power of Imagination?

Cultivate your Imagination.

People do the things they first see done with their Imagination. McAdoo with the eye of his mind saw rapid cars taking thousands of people daily under the Hudson river. Of course, people turned their heads and smiled at his dream. But McAdoo made real his dream in the Hudson tunnels. Marconi saw the messages of people thousands of miles away floating on the wave of the air and sounded off at a marvelous instrument. He was at once rated as crazy. But he went ahead and presented to an astonished world the unbelievable Wireless telegraph!

Cultivate your Imagination.

People call America the "land of Opportunity." It is the land of Imagination. Herd the humblest rises to the greatest position of power. It's the working of Imagination that contributes most. The obscure clerk sees himself President of the concern he serves. Then he advances step by step until he realizes his aim. His first step toward the President's job was to see himself with his Imagination, occupying it.

Cultivate you Imagination.

The great Perthes once said that "a quick Imagination is the salt of earthly life, without which nature is but a skeleton; but the higher the gift the greater the responsibility."

Cultivate your Imagination.

Cultivate it in little things. Then the little things will become big things. Then the big things will take their place among the undying things. History is but the story of the achievements of people who had Imagination.

Cultivate your Imagination.

Ghosts

THERE is nothing in Ghosts. But they do exist. Ghosts are nothing more nor less than the phantom Imaginations of sick, afraid Minds. They go by various names — Failure Ghosts, Idea Ghosts, Mistake Ghosts, Chance Ghosts, Regret Ghosts — and Millions of others.

Pace your Ghosts.

Walk right up to your Ghosts. Shake hands with them. Look them in the eye. Give them a hearing. And then kick them out — for they never will do you any good.

Face your Ghosts.

Ghosts are always on the Job. In the office of the Doctor, Lawyer, Business man, in your Home, on the Street — everywhere. But Ghosts get uneasy in the Light. They are born and bred in the Dark Alleys and exist only by the Sandbag. Your cue is to keep the Lights turned on — your Mind open — your Courage alert, your Character Impregnable.

Face your Ghosts.

Today when you read your newspapers there will be Ghosts between the Lines of the Print. Ghosts seek you out and constantly try for your scalp. They like Time-Wasters, The Man-Afraid-of-His-Job Hesitaters. They revel among the players of idle Good-fellowship. But Ghosts sneak like cowed dogs with their tails between their legs, at the sight of Doers, Time Users, Obstacle Riddlers, and Path Makers. Be unafraid of Ghosts.

Face your Ghosts.

But don't harbor them. Live, Red-Blooded Men can't be dragging around a lot of Ghosts and amount to Anything.

Face your Ghosts.

Respect

RESPECT is the name of the Fellow who tends door for your Conscience. His is the most sacred Office in the gift of your Character. For, when he goes wrong, Conscience becomes ill unto Death. Nothing of Winning matters with Respect gone. Respect is your most faithful Friend, your greatest

Guide, your most powerful Protector — your safest Pilot into Port.

Nothing of Winning matter with Respect gone.

And Respect is made at home. You are your own Respect. For a man can be on no better terms with anybody than with his Own Self. The Man without Respect is a Make-believe, a Fraud — a Counterfeit.

Nothing of Winning matters with Respect gone.

Respect yourself and other people will be compelled to Respect you — and you will Respect them. Respect is the beginning of Wisdom. With Respect on guard, you look people squarely in the Eye without wavering. With Respect, active and unafraid, you go ahead to move away Rubbish and Obstacles and pave a Path for other people to walk in from which they profit.

Nothing of Winning matters with Respect gone.

Think about this as you move about Today. Let it keep you Strong. Let it make you indomitable. Let it lift you from your present position into one higher up. Let it make of you a Leader. For —

Nothing of Winning matters with Respect gone.

General Manager

HUMAN beings were created to run themselves. Else at birth, each would have been accompanied by a Book of Instructions. You are your own General Manager. Realize but this and it will make you thrill with Fire and Force.

Are YOU on the Job?

No one else can possibly see your Faults in the clear light that you yourself can see them. No one else can possibly fathom the Mysteries of your Mind so thoroughly. No one else can possibly supplant your ability to powerfully picture your own great Ideals and Purposes. No one else can possibly dictate the Policies and Measures of your own life so well. No one else can possibly so efficiently get Work and Results from your marvelous Brain and Body machinery. Who's conducting your shop, anyway? You are the General Manager.

Are YOU on the Job?

Most of us are just First, Second, Third, etc., ASSISTANT General Managers. We let someone else do our Thinking for us. We want the fancy Titles and Glory — but shirk at doing the work.

Are YOU on the Job?

If not, do this without delay. Call a meeting of your own Intellectual Faculties. Insist on a full meeting. Then lock the door and get down to Business. Take your seat at the head of the table. Discuss frankly and freely the Real Things that concern your life Success. But keep solidly in mind that you are the Boss — the Force behind all the Artillery, the real Directing Factor — the actual General Manager.

Lincolnize

A man is always bigger than anything big that he does. No man will ever be able to create any- thing greater than his own Character. To take a single illustration — Lincoln. To Humanity, Abraham Lincoln is infinitely finer than President Lincoln, and as the years accumulate, deeper and deeper do his superb qualities penetrate into the innermost workings of the peoples and nations of the world.

Lincolnize your Work.

The rules of action that guided Lincoln were the rules of ordinary Sense and Humanity. They were tin-varnished. They were disguised by no extra trappings and encumbrances. The simplest thinking person immediately grasped the just rulings and conclusions of Lincoln. The best investment that any Business House can make is to gather together the simple rules of conduct that guided Lincoln, and have them Printed, Framed and Hung, before the faces of every one of its Employees.

Lincolnize your Business.

When Lincoln promoted General Hooker he told him that he was doing it in spite of the fact that he had glaring Faults, Enemies, Vanities, and a lot of other

things. Lincoln recognized the high qualities of Leadership that Hooker had and he was not blinded by his defects. He always saw the Big things in a man. He knew Grant even before he had met him. He felt men by their Deeds. Results to him reflected the man.

Lincolnize your Judgment.

Lincoln was Just. Lincoln was Generous. Lincoln was Square. Lincoln was Magnanimous. Lincoln was Modest. Lincoln was Gentle. Lincoln was Strong.

Lincolnize your Ideals.

System

BE Systematic.

The Thought, the Plan, the Energy, the Success of your day is measured in value by your application to each — of System.

Be Systematic.

First, it is the easiest way. And then, it is the only way. For without System, the most stupendous Task is sure to crack, crumble and fall into a wreck of waste and loss.

Be Systematic.

With System, a worthwhile Purpose, and an iron determination, progress is steady and smooth and sure. Difficulties fade away. Obstructions are pushed aside, and the Completed Task rises with precision and reality, like unto the rising shafts of steel that reach skyward, outlining and suggesting and making real the giant form of the completing Skyscraper. All through System!

Be Systematic.

Form the habit of undertaking even the smallest Task through System. Then the big things will be achieved with ease and with enjoyment.

Be Systematic.

But don't be satisfied to apply System to yourself alone. Teach it to others. You who are a Stenographer, Clerk, Manager, Owner of a Business — no matter what your niche — see that System rules your Throne.

Be Systematic.

Sincerity

BE Sincere.

For it's the mark that stamps and "Trademarks" your Character so that it stands at once as Genuine.

Be Sincere.

Nobody trusts the man who doesn't trust himself. Be Sincere. Look the other fellow in the eye squarely and with confidence, and he will trust you.

Be Sincere.

Lacks in ability and knowledge are many times excused. But insincerity — never. Be Sincere. Teach the world once for all that you are square — Sincere — and the "order of business" for you will move smoothly and with satisfaction.

Be Sincere.

Sincerity is more than money. Even as the magnet attracts and clusters to itself particles of steel, so does the man who holds Sincerity as his asset, draw Men and Chances and great Works to his record.

Be Sincere.

Trouble yourself not that Yesterday was a failure. Today faces you. Try a new instrument. Tighten new cords for a new Tune. Take hold on a new Force — be Sincere. Then will this day have been far from in vain.

Be Sincere.

Dig

DIG.

Dig right through every obstacle. Fight to uphold the dignity of your Purpose. Dig, bore, squeeze, sweat — but get through!

Dig.

The regular, persistent drop of water will wear away the hardest stone. Science says that the even, rhythmic step of an army has power to start the wreck of the strongest bridge. In like manner does determined effort win anything — anywhere. To believe so, start today to —

Dig.

Dig! You see the other fellow carrying away plenty of Bacon? Dig. You failed in many things yesterday? Dig. You want money, reputation, glory? Dig. Mental, moral, or financial Bankruptcy stares boldly at you? Pay no attention. Just —

Dig.

Success is not a thing inherited. To get it you must —

Dig.

Dig.

Every man or woman who ever won at anything knew how to — Dig. It is the "A" word of the Alphabet of Doing. Dig. No matter WHAT you want or WHERE you want it, or WHEN you want it, you must first know how to Dig — or you won't get it. Dig.

Dig.

Concentrate

CONCENTRATE.

With steadiness, courage, dare-determinedness burn a hole into things. No matter what the thing at hand may be.

Concentrate.

The Wheel of Action and of Business moves by steady turns around one central hub. In Success, Rim, Spoke, Hub hold tight together, and as though human, Think, Plan, Move as one.

Concentrate.

Results come always to the persistent. Opportunity goes out of its way to get hold of the hand of the Sticker. The eye of the Boss is drawn irresistibly to the desk of the Doer. Concentrate.

Concentrate.

Draw the details together. Formulate your day's Plan. Strike a pace. Make every minute and every move count. Concentrate. And the finished Job will be the day's Goal — twenty-four hours of life well worth while.

Concentrate.

Learn

BE an Observer. Let nothing new appear without first clinching its value, studying its meaning, and absorbing its lesson. Learn.

Find Out.

Learn from Nature, People, Happenings. Read the thought of each day as far as you can fathom. Then apply your Knowledge. Learn all the time from everything you can — everywhere. Investigate the Mysteries, master the Difficulties.

Find Out.

Right now — a paragraph from History. John Milton — a word from you. "I am blind, past fifty, but I am completing my 'Paradise Lost'." Michael Angelo — your testimony. "Though seventy years of age, I am still learning." John Kemble — what have you to say? "Since leaving the stage, I have written out Hamlet thirty times. I am now beginning to understand my art!" You who have eyes, and ears, and mouths to talk with — Learn.

Find Out.

Your work today may look useless. You may be "only a Clerk." But you will always be one if you fail to Learn. For the Path of advancement marks the Way of the man. Learn.

Find Out.

Leadership comes solely to those who KNOW. Knowledge is surely Power. The Diners at the Table of the Feast of Success are no favored folk — none other than those who took the time to Learn. You — if you would Win — Learn!

Think

PEOPLE are paid, ambition is achieved, success comes only in the measure that a man Thinks.

Think.

All great Doers were and are great Thinkers. Think. Mistakes, Confusion, Consternation are rare callers at the brain of the man who Thinks.

Think.

But think to a definite purpose. Systematize your ideas. Plan out the acts of each of your minutes, and hours — and days. Think.

Think.

Napoleon was a Thinker. Sought out one day in one of the crises of France, he was found in an obscure garret, studying the streets of Paris and Thinking out his best moves for the morrow. Think.

Think.

Be your own Silent partner. Think. Be responsible to your own Intellectual Force. Think. Forge from the anvil of your own hard fights and failures, the Deeds of Doing that can only come after the most rigid and painstaking Thoughts. Think.

Think.

Start this day with the resolve to Think out each act you perform, knowing that the largest and most useful Results follow the man who Thinks.

Opportunity

OPPORTUNITY is a Something — not a nothing; also, something Real — not a Phantom. And, too, Opportunity is an Ever-present — here today and here tomorrow. By moments, hours, days, weeks, months — years, she hovers about, unseen and unheard — except as her Spirit is felt and — seized!

Opportunity is the hand of Progress to the alert, and the "handwriting on the wall" of Failure, to the groggy and the slothful. For of all Messengers of Light she — Opportunity — is the one most patient, most fair, most just and most considerate.

Opportunity is no respecter of persons or of seasons. She is ever on the job and she ever waits and waits and waits. The man may fall forever asleep — but Opportunity — never.

At this actual minute she stands before YOU. All through the livelong day she will be at your call. Lightning-like she flashes her Messages to all — but her sole appeal is — to you.

Think How about it? "Stop, look, listen" — can you see, hear, feel, grip her hand? Make the most of what she holds this day for you. Think — think, think!

Then ACT.

For Opportunity, converted into a Fact, is the taking hold on the simplest task at hand — and doing it to a finish in the best way you know how. It's picking up the pins of Priceless Minutes that the other fellow passes heedlessly over. It's doing your work BETTER than you are paid for, and tackling bigger jobs than you may think you are capable of handling.

Great is the rise of the man who makes an early friend of Opportunity and takes her with him through the paths of the common every day.

Loyalty

BE Loyal.

To be Loyal is to be square with yourself. And you cannot be square with yourself without being a pretty good sort of a Boss — of yourself. The trouble with the people that fail is that they let someone else run their shop. Then disloyalty creeps in and sours and sucks and saps the life of a man away from himself.

Be Loyal.

You know your own possibilities better than any living being. Get next to them without delay and learn to be Loyal to them. It's a quality beyond price — this Loyalty.

Be Loyal.

The Loyal man oft times is of all men with discouragement tempted. But the fellow who sticks to his Faith and is Loyal — is the man that finally feels Growth and Equipment and Power becoming a part of himself.

Be Loyal.

Loyalty means sacrifice. But sacrifice means Success!

Be Loyal.

The steps of Achievement and Honor and Satisfaction are all rock riveted to Loyalty — Loyalty to your Work, and to your Friends.

Be Loyal.

Benefits redound to the fit and worthy. Your work today may seem mean and obscure indeed to yourself. But "the gods see everywhere" and the least neglect or slight to what you hold in hand today, may reflect and loom large in the completed work. Loyal attention from the start to the finish is the safest, fairest and surest path for you to pursue. Do but this and Results will take jealous care of you.

Be Loyal.

Courage

HAVE COURAGE.

Courage is the art of sitting calmly in your seat without stirring and without getting excited when the Brass Band of Popularity, or Temporary Success or Ridicule goes by your house and turns around the corner. Courage steps out of the crowd. It stands alone.

Courage is native Nerve — refined.

Courage is neither bulldozing nor bare bluff — it's not related to either. Courage isn't physical merely, but moral — mostly.

Courage is naked Right put through fire and brought out uncracked and unbroken.

Courage is heart worth making itself felt in deeds. It never waits for chances; it makes chances.

A day without some Courage sprinkled in it is a day little worth while. For Courage makes the Man — and there never was a real Man that didn't have Courage.

Courage is a thing born in you — but it is also a thing much lustered by use and cultivation.

Today, tomorrow — and every day — have Courage. It makes the heart glad and the soul strong. It starts smiles in the system and stirs up the kind of circulation in a man that makes him go out and do his best at the most humble undertaking.

You can never fail if you have Courage — but you can never win without it.

Have Courage!

Fight

LEARN to be a Fighter.

Not with fists or clubs or swords — but through the noble mastering of the Forces at your command — generated by your own Brain.

For great are victories gained from the everyday battles of life over the endless difficulties that almost hourly face such a Force.

Learn to be a Fighter.

Then fight! Fight face to the front — fiercely yet fairly. And when everybody looks upon you as a loser and calls you whipped — that's your cue to finish the fight — and WIN!

Learn to be a Fighter.

You will not always win, but never admit it. Half the so-named failures of all time lie in Conquerors' graves. And the flowers of God, and the winds of undying Fame cool and smooth the sleeping souls that didn't know HOW to die!

Learn to be a Fighter.

What is your work today? Make it a battle front! Muster the best that is in you and go out to meet and vanquish every obstacle that seeks to keep this day from being the one you will most prize as the one of all your days most worth while — to other people and to yourself. Fight every inch of the way. Give no quarter — and accept none. Go to your bed with the spirit and satisfaction of a Conqueror.

Learn to be a fighter!

Stick

STICK.

Just Stick.

This is the essence — the beginning and ending — of Success.

Stick.

The Sticker is the "get there" man.

Stick.

Everybody begins — but not all Stick. Yesterday you failed, maybe, but today you can Win — if you Stick it out. All achievers wear a badge labeled "STICK."

You Stick — today.

When you feel like quitting — Stick! If the other fellow is getting the best of you — Stick. He will if you don't.

Stick.

The great successes of business and life are but repetitions of the same story — the story of men who knew HOW to Stick.

Stick.

You may not like your job, but think before you change it. So few know HOW to Stick. So few learn WHEN to Stick. So few care WHERE they Stick. You think it out with patience. Then — whether it be a job or a task — Stick it out.

Stick.

Today — start things and Stick to each until finish! — completed in the best way you know how.

Just Stick.

Faith

HAVE Faith.

First, Faith in yourself, then Faith in the thing you set out to do — then Faith in the result.

Faith is the ability to believe you have won before you have. It's the art of beating the enemy, the obstacles, or the plan of your opposers, before they have securely organized. For Faith is to take victory in hand at the start.

Have Faith.

The great stories of Success from the beginning of time are but narratives of men and women doers — who had Faith. Faith feeds the hungry in adversity — clothes and warms the needy in temporary failure. For Faith builds. It cannot destroy.

Have Faith.

Your success is limited only by your Faith. The results from Faith live limitless. Take heart.

Have Faith.

The only time people fail is when they lose Faith. The Pitcher in a ball game, the Soldier on a battle-field, the Leader in Politics, the Executive at the head of a task or business — the humblest Toiler — each goes ahead and does his best only as he is inspired to it by Faith. First, as he has it — then as those about, under or near him have Faith in him.

Have Faith.

And make it a vital part of your determination to Win, today. The most obscure worker is entitled to as great credit for results in proportion, as the man who commands — so long as he has and uses all the Faith he can muster. So, remember to keep a good stock of Faith on hand constantly. All this day long —

Have Faith.

Enthusiasm

ENTHUSIASM is what happens to a man when on taking invoice, he discovers that his Heart and Head and Determination have finally welded into and become a part of "the Main Chance."

Enthusiasm is a process — not merely a condition.

Almost everybody has a Head and Heart and Determination — but it's the folks that have sufficient sense to get these together in the same spot at the same time for the same purpose that start things and move on the progress of the times.

Enthusiasm is the spark that starts the Action that moves the Man that finds the Cows and brings them home. Enthusiasm is what makes a fellow "get there."

Get Enthusiasm and you will "steam on." Nobody can stop you.

Enthusiasm is what goes through stone walls, bores miles under great rivers, wins battles and lays out cities and towns and nations. Enthusiasm changes maps and makes History possible.

You at your desk, at your plow, at your broom, at your axe, at your bat, at your pen — you, no matter who or where you are — take heart and hope and Enthusiasm.

For Enthusiasm starts things, shapes things — does things.

Start today to mix Enthusiasm in your blood.

Then keep it there!

Do

Do. The Doer is the digger — and the digger is the Builder.

Do.

The Doer is the mover — and the mover is the Winner.

Do.

Do the things you start, Do the thing you have at heart, Do what the other fellow can but doesn't; Do while there's time, Do while there's life, and Do while there's hope; Do for your own sake, Do because you love to, Do because you must. Do, because this is the way to start — to Win!

Do.

Do the job at hand — for the job moves on. Do when it shines and Do when it rains. Do through the frowns and Do through the smiles. Do on your legs and Do at your desk. Do after you've failed and Do after you've won. But no matter whether early or late, whether here or there — Do.

Do.

And Do it Now — Do it To-day.

Do.

I Will

I WILL — make this day Worth While. I will drop the Past, remembering it only as a valuable path through which I have walked into the Now. I will take up the work of this day as a personal Pledge to do my best — with interest and enthusiasm. I will do the things I have failed to do before. I will attempt new things that I know now that I can do. I will go ahead.

I will play the game today with a warm heart and a cool head. I will smile when I feel like frowning. I will be patient when I feel tempted to scold. I will take personal command of myself.

I will be loyal to the concern for which I toil. I will be faithful to all my trusts. I will master the smallest detail. I will boost — not knock. I will do — not intend. I will get things done.

I will work because I like to. I will be fair and just because there is no other way — to Win. I will do right because it is right. I will drink defeat, if it comes at times, as good medicine. I will sweat by courageous effort — determined to succeed at all times.

I will be careful of my Time, considerate of my Health, jealous of my Honor. I will help make this day great for everyone with whom I come in contact. I will work for the people whom I serve with all my heart and with all my mind and with all my strength. For in the glory and success of my concern is hidden the glory and success of my own self.

I will make this day Worth While.

Smile

SMILE!

The face that Smiles is the face that every one is looking for — and wants. Smile. For the Smiler is the Climber — and the Smiler is the Winner. Smile.

If doubt and defeat drub you at times — Smile. Smile. If it rains when you think it ought to shine — Smile. Smile. Start Smiles. Smile. The Smiling Worker is the Smiling Doer. Smile.

Smile.

More things have been wrought and brought through Smiles than this world dreams of. Smile. A Failure doesn't want to Smile — and can't. A Winner wants to Smile — and can't help it. Smile.

Smile.

Smiles beget Smiles. Smile. Smiles warm the blood, stiffen the back and start courage anew. Smile.

Smile.

Smile when you wake. Smile. Smile when you go and Smile when you come. Smile. Smile when you start your work and Smile when you end it. Smile. For Smiles keep the livelong day from going stale. And Smiles keep the well from going dry. Smile.

Smiles are the headlights of Success. And they always point the way that wins the day.

Smile.

Grit

GRIT is getting the Brain and Heart and Soul of a man fused for a concerted, white-hot attack on Failure.

Grit is what grasps at the raw edge of Victory and chews it to the point of easy digestion. And Grit wins — it gets there!

Grit started the action of the world — and has moved things ever since. Grit lost — all is lost.

Grit is what keeps us from becoming beggars — helps us to shake hands heartily with Progress. Grit is the maker of Masters that master all things. Grit drives the stakes that point the path. Grit is what keeps a fighting man from goirg "stale."

Grit "brings home the bacon."

Grit make the way for the Worker and the Doer. Grit is the pivot on which the aims and ideals and hopes of fighters hang steadily unto Success.

No sweat, no sweet — no Grit, no Glory.
So — get Grit!

Chances

GRASP your Chances as they come. For it's the approaching of the Goal — just ahead — the turning of the Chance into the Achievement, that stirs and spurs the striving man to the fought out fact of the thing dreamed about, planned about — and done.

Take advantage of the smallest chance.

First see it. Then grasp it! Then bolt it to your very soul. Remembering that Chances seen — and secured — breed Ideas, mould the Characters of mighty Men and make Success sure.

Master the trivial. And the big things will loom into Deeds, perfectly plain, exact — undertakable. Especially is this true of the beginner of big things starting small. Deeds done determine, the value of the Chance seized by the man.

The large tasks of the world lie hidden underneath the smallest Chances sought for with calm Patience and cool Courage. If past Chances appear neglected, passed by, or not seen, the future Chances streak toward you from in front — or maybe latent — but ready. Seek them, find them. Then hold them — "for keeps."

Success follows the Chances nailed down — things done.

You — today — go after the Chances. Take them, ruddy and new, and build from this day, things worthwhile and things for more than today.

Grasp your Chances as they come.

Conscience

BE Square.

The man of all men most miserable is the man with a worn, weary, weeping Conscience.

Be Square.

Conscience is the fellow who sits on the throne of your Soul and calls out the Danger Signal when your life craft sights Icebergs. Conscience is the pilot of a man's Hope toward Success. Conscience is the Busy Signal sign that halts a man just as he is about to do what he ought not to but wants to.

Be Square.

Conscience is the Voice of Duty — in every day clothes.

Be Square.

Conscience is what you feel but do not hear. Conscience is the still, strong, silent, unseen Force that is ever with you — that invariably hunches you in the ribs — mute warner that you are on the wrong track, traveling in the wrong direction, playing the wrong game. Regardless of all other heeds, beck or call — hear, listen to — obey your Conscience to the letter.

Be Square.

The Man with the Conscience makes the Business with a Conscience. The Business with the Conscience makes the Nation with the Conscience. Conscience in Power is real achievement.

Be Square.

As a Man or Woman, think it over. Conscience to you is as no other Conscience to any other Man or

Woman. And the height to which Peace and Power may climb in you can be only in proportion to the Peace and Power which obedience to Conscience brings. So, follow your own Conscience all the way.

Be Square.

Promptness

BE on Time.

Because of the lateness of Marshal Grouchy of the French army at the battle of Waterloo, Blucher had time to whip his army on to the help of Wellington. Napoleon ordered rightly. Had not the man to whom he entrusted those orders blundered — hesitated — been Late — the whole history of Europe would have been changed from 1815.

Be on Time.

"The Train was late," is the most frequent explanation after a terrible accident. What a multitude of lives have been lost, what an army of men and women have been deprived of position and honor, what untold suffering and humiliation have followed in the path of the late Mr Late. Nothing pays better than Promptness.

Be on Time.

Promptness is the act of being on the job when your name is called — and answering to it. Not NEARBY — but THERE.

Be on Time.

Time tolls its minutes with even, regular strokes. The Job, the Appointment, the Order, the Friend, the Opportunity — won't wait for the man who doesn't respond on the dot.

Be on Time.

Be not deceived by the cheap clanging of Gold and Silver — gifts through whose possession you imagine yourself immune to Honor and the Promptness of Appointments. There is no winning to the slothful. The world with all its wonderful offerings gives its Choice freely to the man of his word.

Be on Time.

Be on Time at your desk each day — at each and every Appointment throughout each day. The path to greatness starts by being on time each morning at your own Breakfast table. That's the beginning, anyway.

Be on Time.

Thoughts

THOUGHTS are what happen when your Brain gets busy. Also, Thoughts are the Servants sent out by your Mind to shape and complete Deeds.

Feed your Thoughts the right Food.

Thoughts are never inherited. Thoughts are individual and belong wholly to you who create them. So, in turn, you are responsible for them. Care for them with zeal. Keep them Clean and Wholesome.

Feed your Thoughts the right Food.

Thoughts are the Master Builders of Fate. And as sure and plain as the chisel in the hands of the Sculptor

leaves the lines and form of the finished Statue, so do Thoughts cut and shape your Character — and no man can change their work. Thoughts are Messengers of Events.

Feed your Thoughts the right Food.

Train your Thoughts. Organize them. Concentrate them. Exercise them. Guard them. Glory in the Society of your Thoughts — alone. For your Thoughts are your best Companions. Besmirch them — betray them, and you loom useless and abandoned.

Feed your Thoughts the right Food.

As your Mind grows in Strength, your Thoughts increase in Power. It is a wise plan, therefore, to fill your Mind with Thoughts that inspire and cheer and ennoble. For in the darker days of stress and rebellion that come into every life, the re-enforcements of great and useful Thoughts, step out to Protect and Save.

Boost

THERE are a great many people on this earth that we don't need and that we wish we could just easily push off. Knockers, for instance. There is a difference between a Knocker and a Kicker. Sometimes people kick to a good purpose. But a Knocker is a Knocker — a Pest and a Destroyer. Here is the way to push the Knockers into Oblivion —

Boost!

Boost your Town. Boost your Business. Boost your Friends. Boost your Ideas. Boost everything that helps other people or yourself. Be a Booster and you can't help but be a Builder.

Boost!

The man who Boosts is a Leader. He is always followed by a crowd. His philosophy at once becomes contagious. He leaves a trail of Boosters in his path. While those who follow him cut his name into Bronze.

Boost!

When you don't know what else to do — Boost. It makes little odds what you Boost so long as you Boost something. Once you form the habit you need have no fear for lack of things to Boost. They will spring up from every direction.

Boost!

If you want to be happy — Boost. If you want to get higher in the world — Boost. The Busiest and Wisest men that live will be glad to listen to you if you are a Booster. Learn the knack of Boosting. It's a great knack — more important than any "Pull," or "Influence" — and it's bigger than the mere making of Money.

The Battle

THE greatest Battles being fought anywhere are those you fight daily inside your own Soul — against Anger, Lies, Habits, Misjudgments, Ill Health — Circumstances. Continually it is The Battle.

The Battle — to find out how far Brain and Body fiber can be put to the test in order to learn that The Man is in Command.

Heroes pass us daily — and we know it not.

Character and Strength come from Strife. Like the Diamond, you become valuable only after the most painstaking toil and effort. We all come up out of the rough — we all demand cutting and polishing and shaping before we are able to stand out beautiful and inspiring.

But Battling should hold nothing of gloom and sourness. For even in Defeat, there is always something Won. The main requisites are to keep Smile-bound, carry light Equipment, and in the words of Cromwell, " trait in God and keep your Powder dry."

Welcome The Battle, as it goes on in your life. Plan each little Skirmish with Care and with Courage. Be unmindful of the outside Crowd. Center on the destroying forces that face you and fight them to a finish. Then get ready for another Battle. Charge the dissenters in your own ranks. But keep your face toward the Enemy, under whatever name it fights you.

Always Battle to Win!

By firmly and patiently loading and reloading the guns at your command you become a seasoned Soldier. Little by little the intricate rules and principles of warfare become more ample and understandable. You begin to feel yourself a Leader and a Conqueror.

Thus does The Battle — fought out by us hourly with fortitude — make real Men and Women of us all.

Appreciation

APPRECIATION is the Salt that savors the work and life of the World. Without Appreciation for what we do and without Appreciation for what is done for us, the merest task would become a burden and the Sunshine would go down out of the Hearts of People.

Express your Appreciation.

Appreciation is often withheld for fear of an advantage being taken of it. Nothing could be more foolish. Such a man takes advantage of himself. Appreciation acts like oil on the dry, worn parts of a machine. It starts off everybody and everything with Smiles. Continued Appreciation keeps things running smoothly. Also it saves wear.

Express your Appreciation.

People waste away, render but half service, and finally drop back in the race simply through a lack of Appreciation. Appreciation is not only one of the most powerful Tonics on earth — it's an actual necessary Food. And without it no one partakes of a Balanced Diet.

Express your Appreciation.

If you are an Employer and one of your Helpers does good work, tell him so. And if you are a Helper and your Employer encourages you on, tell him so in thanks and increased service. Appreciation stirs and stimulates. It goes to a man's soul as an electric current to the sensitive nerve centers.

Express your Appreciation.

Appreciate the chance to Live. Appreciate your Health, your Home, your Father and Mother, your Friends, your Opportunity. Some of these you may not have. But Appreciate what you do have — and greater gifts will hourly be added. Up FOR general Run-down-edness try the Tonic — "Up." The "Up" Tonic has actually saved this big world from going off to a Hospital. Millions daily rise to sing its marvelous praises.

Get Up

That is the first step. Stand Up. The more you test your own Strength, the more you will pat yourself on the back for having such Strength. Get Up — and stay Up.

Cheer Up.

The Best is always yet to come. Cheer Up. All you have to do is to go after the Best. And then, Cheer is so Magnetic. No matter where you work or where you go — you draw People and Fortune your way. Suppose the Cow did kick over the pail of Milk. There's more Cow and there's more Milk. Cheer Up!

Smile Up.

Smiles don't count when they hit the ground. Smile Up.

When you face a day that seems knotted with kinks, Smile Up. There will be very few Kinks left. At every time and in every place — Smile Up. Make no exception. Smile Up.

Climb Up.

Be satisfied with nothing. Climb Up. Gather up carefully and patiently the threads of Toil and Experience that make up your completed day and use them as a Rope with which to pull yourself higher. Climb Up.

Lift Up.

If everybody were always Up and never Down, there would be no reason for this little Talk. Somebody is always Down and somebody is always Up. You who are Up help the one who is Down. Lift Up. Then

YOU will be HIGHER Up.

Lead

THIS world needs Leaders more than it needs any other breed of men. Every line of activity calls for Leaders — every Home, every Business, every Town — every Nation. As long as there are people there will be plenty to Follow. The demand is for those who can Lead.

Be a Leader.

The greatest asset in Leadership is Courage. Cowards never Lead. Leadership requires great Patience. No one will follow an Irritable or Impatient Leader. Leadership requires Tact, Fairness and Confidence. One man can't Lead another who distrusts his Leadership. Many other things are important — but these things are Imperative.

Be a Leader.

A Leader must inspire and wake up the sleeping

POWERS in his followers. He must be able to draw out, into action, the very highest qualities of people. To be able to do this he must himself have a clean consistent Record. A man can't command without Authority — a man can't stir other people without first having stirred himself and become his own Master.

Be a Leader.

It is just as important to be a Leader in your own Home or Town as to be a Leader in your Country. It isn't the special station in which a man Leads that makes his work most important but it's HOW he Leads. This thing is true — that if you Lead well in the little affairs of life you can't keep from becoming a Leader in the big affairs.

Be a Leader.

Vision

VISION is Act-seeing. Great Vision means that you see things DONE by way of your Imagination, even before they are attempted. Vision differs from Imagination. It starts from Imagination. Imagination takes the Pictures but Vision turns them over to the Architects who Build things from them. Men with Vision are Dominant.

Look Out.

Muster your Ideas. For Ideas germinate Vision. They give it Flesh and Blood, Feed its Fire Box, Control its Nerves — Pump its Heart. Ideas make Vision a living thing.

Look Out.

Despise Vision and you become a Hireling — dependent and owned. Court Vision and you become a Master — a Wielder of Power unlimited. Vision is Optimism with two healthy Eyes.

Look Out.

Vision comes to, and may be gained by, the humblest. It carries neither a Patent nor a Copyright. It's a "tramp" element in the sense of freedom. But it must be sought, found — and then fed and clothed. Vision comes to no one unhunted.

Look Out.

Your Vision is Big or Little as you will it. The greater you aspire the greater will grow your Vision. The farther you See — the more you will Do. Vision is applicable to the everyday. It puts strength back of effort. It brings Permanence to your acts.

Look Out.

Dampers

DAMPERS are Checks. They are also Savers. Attached to a heating apparatus, they Check the draughts and Save the fuel. Human beings have Dampers. Thought itself is a Damper — also Judgment, Conscience, Expediency — and many others. No one, however, can ever know your own Dampers so well as you Yourself. But —

Know WHEN to use your Dampers.

Dampers are very Essential. An open Damper on a Furnace might so heat things as to cause an Explosion or a Fire. On the other hand it might be so turned off as to put out the Furnace, entirely. So, exactly, is it true in regard to the Dampers that go to regulate and make up your modes of Action — and your Character.

Know WHEN to use your Dampers.

Study your Draughts. A few of them are Enthusiasm,

Energy, Will, Learning — Money. There is a Damper for every Draught. If used intelligently increased results are secured. If Enthusiasm sweeps you out of the Practical — turn on the Reason Damper. If you go into things with nothing but a Will to go through — turn on the Thought Damper. Don't Learn so much from Books that you know nothing about Life and People. Remember that you HAVE Dampers. But — Know WHEN to use your Dampers.

And be sure that you use them YOURSELF. Don't let anybody else turn any Dampers on your Enthusiasm, your Ideas, your Plans, your Work. Run your own Dampers. Study them with great care. It's knowing exactly WHEN and HOW to use them that makes the difference between Success and Failure for you.

Bosses

BOSSES are all right — if they are the right Bosses. All through Nature and Human life runs the power of the Boss. Everything would go to smash with a bang if there were no Bosses. That's why it is a satisfying thing to know that —

You can Select your own Boss.

There are Bosses and Bosses. Some people let a little six-inch roll of Tobacco Boss them; some are led around by a harmless looking glass of Liquid Stimulant; some are ruled by a bunch of fool, imaginary Worries; some are commanded by an army of Nerves; some allow an unregulated Stomach to Boss; some call in Clothes and Style and request them to Dictate. Many of these are all right — but none should ever be made Boss.

You can Select your own Boss.

One of the saddest sights in the world is a wrongly

Bossed man or woman. There, germinate all the miseries of the Human. There, Failure drives its stakes. Let's think of OUR Bosses for a minute. Who is your Boss? What Bosses Boss you? Here's something

You can Select your own Boss.

This is the way. Put your WILL in complete control. Make it Boss. The human Will is the greatest and grandest Boss in all the world of Bosses. Nerves! a word with you. YOU are not my Boss. Habit! step out in front. YOU are not my Boss. Appetite! just a moment. YOU are not my Boss. Will! let's shake hands. I Select YOU as my Boss. And from this day on there is to be Order, Growth — Power in this house of mine.

Listen

TO listen is to Learn. Doers of large affairs take very little time to talk — but they are always good Listeners. Anyone may secure a liberal education if he will but take the time to Listen. But it is imperative that you —

Absorb what you Learn.

General U. S. Grant was not a brilliant man. He was a failure in Business. But he set out to become Useful. He was gifted with wonderful determination and doggedness. He had Character. And today, high above the waters of the Hudson, alongside the beautiful Riverside Drive in New York, stands Grant's Tomb — mute testimony to the life and work of Grant, as Soldier and President. So wonderful a Listener was he that while President he became known as "The Silent President."

Absorb what you Learn.

To Listen well is a great accomplishment. No one shows his ignorance quicker than the man who persists in talking without saying anything. If you have some- thing to say — say it. If you have nothing to say — Listen.

Absorb what you Learn.

Select the people to whom you Listen. Listen with respect and an open Mind. Give new Ideas, new Theories and new Programs a hospitable reception, listen well. To you remains the right to reject what you do not want. But always be big enough to Listen.

Then-

Absorb what you Learn.

Let Go

IT takes Courage to start a thing. It takes Courage to stick to a thing. But it takes greater Courage to Let Go of a thing that you are convinced is a Failure, after you have worked and sacrificed and sweat blood to make it Win. But —

Have Courage to Let Go.

The basis of Self-Reliance is Self-Belief. If you consider yourself bigger than your Job — if you feel that you are holding down a $2,500.00 Job with $10,000.00 abilities — Let Go of the $2,500.00 Job and immediately proceed to the $10,000.00 Job.

Have Courage to Let Go.

The principle is the same in Friendship. Nothing stimulates, inspires and leads a man on to Performance, like a Real Friend. But if that Friend lacks the desires that accompany Real Friendship and you are keen enough to discern it — even in Friendship —

Have Courage to Let Go.

Have Courage to Let Go of the little Worries, the little Annoyances — the Trifles, that almost hourly race up to you and plead you to take them in. Think not lightly of these because they are small. It takes a Strong man to kick them out of the way, to pass over them — to abandon them.

Have Courage to Let Go.

The Active Mind draws to itself, like a Magnet, Ideas, Theories and Problems. Some are Useful, some are Useless. When they come to you,

Sift them, Weigh them, Analyze them — take them all apart. Know them for what they are. Then hold to the Useful and drop the Useless.

Have Courage to Let Go.

Clothes

NOTE the man taking care as to his Clothes! he shall shake hands heartily with Success and Success shall take him into Partnership. Clothes may not make the man but a man easily makes his Clothes help make him. They will help you to —

Reveal yourself through your Clothes.

First, Clothes give a feeling of Self-respect. Then it is, however, that the sensible man forgets them. But if he doesn't, then they help to unmake him. Clothes- worship discolors Character and takes from it its luster. For Clothes, after all, are mostly for the Mind. Else we could still dress in skins. Clothes are very accurate indicators to the real Character of a man.

Reveal yourself through your Clothes.

You can do so if you let your Clothes be the means and by no means the end. Clothes and mere Style are of two different Tribes. Neatness and Common Sense in Clothes count most. Shakespeare's advice — "As much as thy purse will allow, neat but not gaudy," is difficult to improve upon.

Reveal yourself through your Clothes.

On the other hand, careful Selection in Clothes, so as to mirror your individuality and personality, becomes one of the most forceful means in your power for your growth. Clothes give prestige. They furnish an "entre." The mental effect of the careful, well-dressed man or woman at once is to stimulate, invite and knit with satisfaction. The great point, however, is to so dress that people become at once interested in

YOU and not your Clothes.

Reveal yourself through your Clothes.

Alone

LEARN to Be Alone. To be Healthily Alone is to be Morally afire. In such Solitude are the Ideas of Centuries hatched. Big minds Think, Decide, Stand — Conquer, while Alone. They self-examine and self-construct.

Learn to Think Alone.

Lincoln was Alone with his pine knots and borrowed books; Hugo was Alone with his mean garrett and pen; Cromwell was Alone at St. Ives behind his plow handle. Wherever great problems or vital decisions have had to be met, men have calmly withdrawn that they might the better weigh everything — Alone.

Learn to Decide Alone.

Emerson says — "Trust thyself: every heart vibrates to that iron string." Can a man trust himself away from himself? Is not the vital test and final greatness of a man all focused on his ability to stand absolutely Alone in emergencies? Props irritate and unnerve. So do irresponsive natures. The Crowd eats away at independence. Real Worth tops like a mountain cap. Nobody can mistake it. Like the mountain itself it stands Alone. No one will ever do for you what you are able to do for yourself — Alone.

Learn to Stand Alone.

If you have personal problems to solve — get Alone. If you are dissatisfied with what you are — get Alone. You will look strangely true to yourself when examined Alone. Nothing stimulates like getting Alone — so long as you get Alone to improve yourself.

Learn to Conquer Alone.

Arbitrate

TAKE the Chip off your Shoulder. One of the surest evidences that this is a time of great Progress is that we are beginning to dig out with great zest from the trunks in our garrets the old-fashioned, dust-covered principles that used to keep us mighty happy before we began to get prosperous.

The package labeled "Arbitrate," for instance.

The meanest human being likes to pride himself on his sense of fairness. It is a fundamental and primitive principle. It was not until somebody got unjust and unfair that Wars and Fighters and Disagreements started. It has always been true that those who "talked it over" in the open soon had things settled and all went back to work.

Arbitrate means to Weigh and Divide. That is, to Weigh the Dispute and Divide the Blame — and then to forget the Dispute.

Fools always fight. Wise people always Arbitrate. Because to fight is to Waste and to Arbitrate is to Save. Sometimes it is money saved, sometimes human beings — but always Character, whether the dispute is between you or somebody else or between a dozen nations.

Arbitrate. Always Arbitrate. It always pays to Arbitrate.

Here's something important. Disputes can never be without Individual Consent. If every person concerned — if YOU — refuse to fight, and the other or others take your "cue," it has to be — Arbitrate. If people would only just think before they get ready to dispute, they would not dispute. Try out this suggestion YOURSELF.

Take the Chip off your Shoulder.

Explore

GOD never put Brains into human heads for mere Fixtures. Brains are just like Continents. They were created to be Explored and Used — to be populated with Ideas. But before you start out on your expedition of Exploration, be sure that you —

Get a Viewpoint.

For next to actual Brains to Work with, there is nothing so important as to have an individual Viewpoint. It is everything to a man. From out of it rises the very Image of a man's life Plan and Ideal. Explore.

Get a Viewpoint.

One man gathers together and puts ready for instant use, the thousands upon thousands of words that make up a Language. We can't forget Webster. He shaped and sharpened the tools — and put them in order. Then

Emerson came along. Poe arrived. Dickens, MacCaulay, Scott — and scores of others stepped up and delved into the tool chest of Webster. Each with his own Viewpoint shaped a literary Career. Explore.

Find out.

Get a Viewpoint.

The whole World is beginning to bare its head to the genius of O. Henry. But marvelous as his words read, they are as nothing to his almost superhuman worked-out Viewpoint. His Pictured People in the cycle of the Humdrum and the Forgotten, will never die until print perishes. He was always Exploring — Exploring.

Get a Viewpoint.

Search, Think, Sacrifice, Study, Travel, Read — get the spirit of Exploration worked into your system. But remember that it is what you GET from Exploring that makes your Expeditions worth while. First —

Get a Viewpoint.

The Cup

THERE are people who actually believe that the best Opportunities have all been lassoed, haltered, and hitched for life to somebody else's front door-post. But the truth is, nobody can corner Opportunity.

For —

Opportunity is Everywhere.

A story is told of a Cup of many Handles. So many handles, in fact, that no matter from what direction a person would approach it, there was a handle to greet him. All that was necessary was to step up and TAKE the handle. like unto this Cup is Opportunity.

Opportunity is Everywhere.

Opportunity is the Cup — and there is a handle in your town. You can grasp it if you will but reach for it. And you need have no fear that somebody else will beat you to your handle — for there is a handle for every single person in your town.

Opportunity is Everywhere.

Not in New York, or Chicago, or San Francisco alone, but in Kokomo, Indiana, Reading, Michigan, and Tacoma, Washington. The handles are everywhere. Just hunt them out and GRASP one and don't let it get away from you. And after you have a handle, lift The Cup and drink from its priceless contents.

Opportunity is Everywhere.

Think of The Cup. Think of its many Handles. When something comes up that ought to be done but that you don't want to do — DO it. That's a Handle. When something happens that takes you from your planned out Task — have no fear. That's a Handle. Get a GRIP upon it. Always look for one of the Handles. And get in the habit of using them. This is the way to learn that —

Opportunity is Everywhere.

Dream

PUT your Dreams to Work. The right kind of a Dream is the Advance Agent of a Deed. Dreams are Pictures of things in the mind that the man of Initiative works out and completes. The world's Doers have always been Dreamers.

Put your Dreams to Work.

But when you Dream, Dream near home. Castles in Cathey can be of no use to you. Dreaming of your neighbor's nicely piled woodshed doesn't saw up your own wood in your own yard.

Put your Dreams to Work.

Plan out your Dreams. And as you have them index them so that you will know where to find them when you want them. Sandpaper them so that you will see what they are made of more clearly. Get them in both your hands and hold them up squarely in front of your face so that you may get their full measure. Then give them a Pick or a Shovel or a Pen. Get them into Action.

Put your Dreams to Work.

Forget your Dreams of Yesterday. Get your Dreams of Tomorrow into work Today. Then Tomorrow they will have grown into Deeds.

Put your Dreams to Work.

Excuses

EXCUSES are little Knock-out Drops that a man uses to Dumbfound and Bedazzle his own conscience on special occasions.

An Excuse never Excuses an Excuse.

People never try to Excuse things that they themselves believe to be right. When you do your Best you are conscious of a Contentment that the very act itself produces. If there is any chance for an Excuse, the thing excuses itself.

An Excuse never Excuses an Excuse.

Your Brain may be unschooled — but the Brain is there. Elihu Burritt probably never was inside a college, but he became famous as the "Learned Blacksmith." He found time in his shop to learn forty languages! He offered no Excuses for an untrained mind. The word Excuse is not in the dictionary of the Willing and the Determined.

An Excuse never Excuses an Excuse.

Did you ever use an Excuse as a prop that it did not fall down? Excuses hamper. Excuses form Stumbling Blocks over which you are sure to fall unless you kick them aside and forget them. Excuses are Unnatural. They wear false faces. They never look to you as they really are. And an excuse never answers anything. The next time you feel like making an Excuse — don't!

For —

An Excuse never Excuses an Excuse.

Envy

YOU who read this little talk, have Things locked up in your Brain that nobody else on earth has or ever has had. And you hold the Key, too. Although the Almighty is in a big business, creating millions of Human Beings, year after year, nobody has ever yet discovered a duplicate Human Being. Every Human Being is an "original." So, if there is any Envying to be done, let the other fellow do it. YOU —

Be too Big to bother with Envy.

Now, Envy is begrudging some other fellow his Good Fortune. To be Envious is to stagnate your own growth. The Envy that you have for the Winning of somebody else takes away in just that measure Winning on your own part. Envy is Self-robbery.

Be too Big to bother with Envy.

Call to your own mind the Big doers. Are they Envious people? No — they are too Busy to Envy. If they took the time to Envy they could not have used their best abilities to Achieve. Be too Big to bother with Envy.

You would never Envy if you would but realize the Accumulated Power that comes by profiting from the Success of other people. Be glad of the Big Luck of somebody else. Be wise enough to let its Inspiration lift you up. Individual Success is not stationary. It has no limitations. Congratulate your friend today and he may be put in the position to congratulate you tomorrow and be happy of the chance.

Be too Big to bother with Envy.

See

THERE are two ways of Seeing. One with the Eyes and one with the Mind. Helen Kellar recently stated in a public address that there were many people more Blind than she. She was right. The Blind are those who WILL NOT see.

Keep your Eyes and Mind wide Open.

Joseph Pulitzer, the late Blind Editor of the New York World, made his newspaper great not until after he became Blind. Prescott wrote his greatest Histories with Sightless Eyes. P. S. Henson, the great Preacher, with but one Eye, has Seen more and learned more than most people would with a dozen Eyes. The Blind many times See most.

Keep your Eyes and Mind wide Open.

Use your Eyes. See Things. And after you See them, make Friends out of them. No two people See Things exactly the same. Watt saw latent Power in the Steam that came out of his mother's Tea Kettle. Franklin saw another kind of usefulness snapping from the tail of his Kite. The followers of these men saw enough to adapt and force Civilization ahead by scores of years.

Keep your Eyes and Mind wide Open.

Many of the really Big Things in this world have not yet been Seen. You, at your humble task Today, may See some of them, or shadows of them. And if you do, persist in Seeing. There is always this one great way to Learn and Grow — to resolve on Seeing everything that can be Seen. But your Eyes are only half. To See with your Mind is the other half.

Keep your Eyes and Mind wide Open.

Hope

HOPE is Heart — in full health. When Hope begins to flicker away, then's the time to flash C. Q. D.

Accumulate Hope.

It is just as easy to become a bankrupt in Hope as to become a bankrupt in Money. Hope is a mixture. It is made up of equal parts of Courage, Will, Work and Faith. Innoculate your system with these things and Hope will hover about you, lead you on, defend you — make you a Factor in the work of the world.

Accumulate Hope.

Perhaps you are one of the people who measure Hope in mere Money, crude Ambition, and flabby Fame. Hope is not material. Hope is Eternal, just like the Stars. And if you are not digging away at a job that has an Ever-living Atmosphere to it, then change your job without delay.

Accumulate Hope.

Hope brightens the Eye, squares the Jaw and stiffens the Backbone. Hope is the invisible picture of Success.

Hope, Hope, Hope —

Accumulate Hope.

Kick

KICK to Grow.

But Kick ahead and not behind. Kick to get Something and to get Somewhere. Kick to a good purpose. For to rightly Kick is to be Somebody.

Kick to Grow.

France Kicked itself into the French Revolution and cleared the Political map of Europe for centuries to come; Wendell Phillips Kicked against human Slavery and helped free a Race; Disraeli Kicked against a great horde of Kickers and it landed him Prime Minister of England. History favors Kickers.

Kick to Grow.

Kick with a Smile on your Face and Determination in your Heart. For the Kicking Business fares badly with Bitterness and Revenge taking tickets at the Gate. Kick the hardest against your own Faults and Defects. Also, Kick against everything useless — Time wasting,

cheap Gossip, aimless People — Habits that sap away your Power.

Kick to Grow.

Kick for recognition when you have real Worth to show. Kick for Knowledge. Kick for Principle. Kick for a place on which to stand squarely and honestly. But in all your Kicking, remember that the Kicking is the Means and not the End. And after you have Kicked your Kick — pass on, and achieve your Task.

Kick to Grow.

U. S.

IN the private Office of the President of one of the greatest of American concerns are these two letters in big, black type on a framed card — U. S. These letters might stand for a great many things. But this is what they actually abbreviate — Universal Spirit.

They also mean to —

Co-operate.

The Universal Spirit makes men Trust each other, makes you want to be Loyal to yourself, to your friends, to your ideals and to your business connections. And, after all, the Universal Spirit is but the great desire to help make things run along smoothly — to get things done without a lot of useless bickering.

Co-operate.

Pear, Friction, Discouragement, Distrust, Disloyalty — each is but the backfiring of a lack of the Universal Spirit. You won't have any strikes in your shop if its motto is the Universal Spirit. To get it, start with the Golden Rule.

Co-operate.

Believe that you have a composite part in what goes to make up the finest part of happiness and you won't need to use the dictionary to define the meaning of the Universal Spirit. It is just to —

Co-operate.

Eliminate

ONE of the greatest gifts of use in the bringing on of Success is the ability to Eliminate. The ability to Eliminate every thought, habit, action that does not contribute and construct toward some useful purpose.

Carry no Dead Wood.

The soldier entering upon his long campaign straps to his back nothing but the lightest equipment — yet he carries everything necessary and every article figures one hundred per cent Efficient.

Carry no Dead Wood.

Why fume and fret and fuss over little annoyances? They are not worth it. Eliminate them. Then step ahead and you will be surprised at your increased agility through lighter equipment.

Carry no Dead Wood.

Here are a few things to Eliminate today — Time Wasting, Bitter Words, Worry over things that never happen, useless spending of Money, the memory of Unintentional Mistakes.

Carry no Dead Wood.

Thoroughness

THIS world is saturated with Human Beings, Jobs, Businesses, Works of Art, Enterprises of Machinery — that are ragged and frayed at the edges, so to speak, because somebody is constantly blundering. Whatever you Do — Do it Well — to the Finish. Failure starts to germinate when you first begin to slight your work. The slight may be ever so small — but be not deceived — at that point your Success begins to die. Whatever you Do — Do it Well — to the Finish.

Have Sense and Courage enough to realize that you will make Mistakes right along. The big thing to Master is the Art of Learning from these Mistakes so that you never make the same ones twice. Conquer every Obstacle that gets in front of you. Win and pass on. Be Thorough.

Whatever you Do — Do it Well — to the Finish.

Nothing that is Worth While is unimportant. And nothing that is important can you afford to neglect or do in a slipshod way. The Employer IS an Employer because he was once a good Employe. Thoroughness is at the bottom of Winning. No structure ever stood — built upon half sand and half stone. Be Thorough — stamping daily upon your very Brain, as a Motto, this thought —

Whatever you Do — Do it Well — to the Finish.

Use

USE! This is one of the most inspiring little words in all the languages of words. Think of what this great America was before men began to use it! A marvelous area, true, but so unhelpful to mankind. But as soon as Thinking Men came and began to Work its Dirt — a Miracle flashed into the face of a sleepy Old World. For —

Use is Growth.

Hang your arm to your side and let it remain there over a long period and it will wither away. Non-use always means Decay, Starvation — Death.

Use is Growth.

You have a Brain — may be as wonderful and as great as any that ever worked. But unless you set to work the little Cells that ache for something to Do, your whole existence will become but an ordinary affair.

Use is Growth.

Do you realize that Distinction which comes to people is simply a matter of Brain Cell Opportunity worked to a Finish — merely taking advantage of every single Chance for advancement — no matter how small the Chance?

Use is Growth.

Your Minutes Used, your Chances Used, your Legs, Arms, Muscles — every Power of Your Body and Brain USED, means a sweeping toward your Purpose that nothing can stop. Those who use what they have and what they get, are the men and women whose names spot History. Do you want to be Somebody? Well, then, remember this —

Use is Growth.

Environment

ENVIRONMENT is Self Atmosphere. Also, it's the invisible Power of Circumstance that always stays around within call. Which is to say, that Environment is the Servant of every man. You can BE Somebody right where you are. Environment is a personal affair. So, if your present Environment hinders you, walk away from it. Hunt out a new Environment. Men and Women who form the habit of getting things done, make their own Environment, hour by hour — day by day.

You can DO Something right where you are.

Bunyan, in Jail, writing the immortal "Pilgrim's Progress"; Milton, blind and domestically all out of kink, penning "Paradise Lost"; John Brown, walking up to the Gallows, smiling, a Prophet of Freedom; Helen Kellar, blind, deaf, dumb, yet the embodiment of Sunshine and Light; these are Masters of Environment!

You can BE Somebody right where you are.

People worthwhile to this world, make their own Environment so attractive that it draws human beings their way. You, who Employ, surround yourself with Cheerful Workers. You, who are Employed, keep your mind saturated with Cheerful Thoughts. Your Environment is what you choose it to be. Add to your Worth Stature.

You can DO Something right where you are.

Worry

IF YOU realized just what Worry is you would stop using it in your business. For Worry is the name given by the Devil to his choicest brand of smelling salts and the more you get into the habit of using them the more you come to know what Hell is really like. Here's an antidote for Worry —

Smile, Smile, Smile — Smile!

For where Smiles are, Worry is not. Worry is just plain poison. It is the most treacherous of poisons for it not only eats into the finest powers of your mind and life but it spreads and radiates like a contagious disease. Worry can do no harm in the atmosphere of cheer, great faith, hope — Work.

Work, Work, Work — Work.

How useless Worry is — how foolish! Realize but this and you will very soon banish it and forever abhor it. Can you think of a single instance where Worry rendered you a service? Well, then, get rid of it.

Smile, Smile, Smile — Smile!

Worry never did and never will bring anything to pass. It never earned a cent and it never helped a human being. But if you keep busy, if you are continually seeking to render some service, you will never have time nor inclination to Worry.

Work, Work, Work — Work.

Grouchers

WHO are they that are the chief Hinderers and Obstructors of the Race — Thieves? No. Anarchists? No. Idlers? No. Grafters? No. Who then? Just these — the Men and Women with a

Grouch.

Be too Busy for a Grouch.

Par the Fellow with the Grouch is the Fellow with a glass of Poison in his hand who will pour it down your throat if you let him. But you will escape him if you will only —

Be too Busy for a Grouch.

A Grouch never helped anything or anybody. And he never failed to do Harm. The Big Man with a Grouch becomes at once a Little Man.

Be too Busy for a Grouch.

Suppose the Grouch does irritate you, suppose he does try to get you off your Guard, suppose he does try to make you "Look Cheap," suppose he does attempt to "Get your Goat." Look him in the eye. Then knock him into smithereens with a 60 h. p. 20th Century model Smile — and Pass On to your Work and your Business.

Be too Busy for a Grouch.

Man-Afraid-Of-His-Job

WE ARE all a bunch of Job holders, no matter the name by which we are known in our work. To work is to be dignified, whether we use a shovel or a pen. There is but one worker in all the drama of work who dishonors the whole profession. He's The-Man-Afraid-Of-His-Job. Get this into your

Head —

YOU are "The Man Higher Up!"

If you will but be this, from this minute you will grow and gather Power. For The-Man-Afraid-Of-His-Job is the man who fears somebody else above him, behind him, alongside of him. He has no Independence for he is all Dependence.

YOU are "The Man Higher Up!"

Results take care of themselves. First be YOURSELF. You may lose your Job. But what of it? You will have then gained a bigger one — Master of Yourself. Cromwell once said that "A man never rises so high as when he does his best not knowing whither he goes." And Emerson says: "Why should we import rags and relics into the new hours?" Keep busy.

YOU are "The Man Higher Up!"

Believe it and proceed. Honor your Job — be it ever so humble — and it will Honor you. Be Positive. Dissolve partnership with The-Man-Afraid-Of-His-Job. Go at your work with the belief that you alone know best your own work and you'll find that it won't take long for others about you to realize for a fact that —

You ARE "The Man Higher Up!"

Encouragement

IF YOU would step into some great seat of Power and Plenty, some day, just get into the Habit of Patting people on the back — with a real Pat of Encouragement.

Give away your own Success.

There is nothing in all the world so stimulating as to feel the thrill of Hope coloring the cheek of some fellow to whom you have just given the Grip of Grit.

Give away your own Success.

Even a Race Horse goes better after a pat on the Nose. The Boot Black gives you a better Polish if you remember to Smile while he Shines. Half the wrecks of life are strewn along the Gutter of Failure for no other reason than this — starved for want of Encouragement.

Give away your own Success.

There are no "Favored of Destiny" Successes. The only Winners are the Favored of Encouragement. The Smile, the hearty Hand Clasp, the sterling Cheer — the cup of Crystal Water — these are the things that make Men, mould Commerce and start to humming Cities and Nations. If you like to Whistle, teach the art to somebody else who dosen't know how.

Give away your own Success.

And, by the way, it is the greatest Fun in all the world! The next fellow to you right now, whoever you are and wherever you are, is just as Human as you are. Turn your pockets of Encouragement inside out.

Keep them empty by giving their contents away — for they will always be full. And, if these little talks help

YOU from day to day, get the knowledge to the fellow who wrote them. It will Encourage him.

Will

JOHN Stuart Mill once said that "a Character is a completely fashioned Will." Which suggests as the greatest task in life — the training and building of the WILL.

Think, not merely, but ACT the Think.

For that is the only sure way to the educated Will. To act with decision, firmness, and promptness when an Emergency arrives is to feed nourishing food hourly to the Will. The weak Will is the starved Will.

Think, not merely, but ACT the Think.

Note the Strong Man. He sees a thing to do and immediately DOES it. The thing may look trivial. It may even seem the work of some other fellow. But without hesitancy, as though dispute was greater than the task, the Strong Man gets the thing Done — so that he may have Time for other and Bigger things.

Think, not merely, but ACT the Think.

The Tragedy of the ten-dollar-a-week Shop Girl, the fifteen-dollar-a-week Clerk, the out-of-a-job Grown Man, is the Tragedy of an untrained Will. The late E. H. Harriman once said: "I am not a ten per cent man!" Which was his way of saying that he was Master of his own Will and a King among Doers.

Think, not merely, but ACT the Think.

Of all things Today that you should not abandon, are the things you least desire to do. For Will building is to do the menial, if necessary, the hum-drum, maybe. But doing everything to a finish as best you can. Knowing full well that a daily mastery of the Little Things worth while makes easy and natural the doing of the Big Things when they come around.

Think, not merely, but ACT the Think.

Harmony

GET in Tune!

We learn our greatest Lessons from Nature. At any hour glance at her Wonders — her Grass, Flowers, Trees, Birds, Rocks. What is the most impressive thing about all these things? This — silent Harmony.

Nature wastes nothing. She quarrels with no one. She dissipates not. Her Team Work is perfect. All her Laws mesh in perfect Harmony. There are no discords.

Get in Tune.

Where there is no Harmony, there is no Progress. Elbert Hubbard gave some great advice when he said: "Get in Line or else get Out!" This ought to be the Motto of this Old World to every one of its Men and Women.

Get in Tune.

There is not a man or business that cannot increase its efficiency over and over again by the application of this simple rule of Harmony — cutting out the Discords — getting back into Accord with the Purpose at hand.

Get in Tune.

Think of the lost Energy and lost Life through your failure to keep in Harmony with your best Thinking or with the Concern that honors you by employing you. Do you realize that what you are carelessly discarding can never be secured again? Stop — this very minute — the leaking of Smiles, high Purposes, big Resolves. Rebellious Thinking cuts into the Heart of your life Force and drizzles it away.

Wake up! There are no dreary days to the Alert —

the Masterful. To you who determine to Win, the story of the Stars and the Planets that do their work in perfect Harmony, is the Inspiration that makes every working minute of Your day Wonderful and Livable!

Get in Tune.

Essentials

DO YOU want to DOUBLE your Efficiency, your Influence, your Results — your very life? Here's a Secret — cut out the NON-essentials.

Give your Time to Things that Count.

Half the "Faithful" Employees, the "Always-to-be-depended-upon" people that fill the Offices and Shops of the land, are nothing more nor less than just "Putterers," and their Employers are too blind to see it. They do their work from day to day — but they take twice the Time necessary and thus WASTE for their Employers one-half.

Give your Time to Things that Count.

Did you ever watch the Doer, the Executive, the Leader — at his job? He instantly sees the BIG things in his Correspondence; immediately he sees the LARGE side of an Employe or of a Problem. Then he dismisses the NON-essentials, and sees that the Essentials are DONE — carried out according to his orders. Such a man is usually the one, too, that does the most and yet always has TIME — for things Worth While.

Give your Time to Things that Count.

Try to pick out the things in your Work Today that really look Essential. Then push aside and away, the useless details. Concentrate on Essentials. For you will never Count in this world unless you —

Give your Time to Things that Count.

Humanism

ISMS are a part of the progress of the race. Here's the best of all — Humanism. Humanism, we will say, is the art of just being Human.

Get back to being Human.

To be Human is to be Yourself, through and through. And anybody that tries to be Human usually tries a lot of things that turn out to be, in the eyes of others who never think of being Human, very silly and very blundering. But that is the delight of it all! The big, strong people are those who are unusually Human.

Get back to being Human.

The Man of Affairs that can see the feeling side of the fellow who puts his coat on; the Woman of Wealth and Society who is able to be Human in the presence of her kitchen girl — they are following out the teaching of Humanism.

Get back to being Human.

Evil Prosperity makes the Snob. Adversity and Catastrophe make the Human.

Get back to being Human.

There are fewer Human beings in Business than there should be. Because men forget that their helpers are not machines, but Blood and Bone and Brain and Heart — and Feeling. If every person who reads this little talk would enter upon his or her work today determined to act like a Human being, think what Happiness would be added to this day! For to be Human is to be Kind, Considerate, Generous, Forgiving, Helpful, Inspiring, as well as to make Mistakes and Err.

Wanted

WANTED — at once — one thousand men of all ages, up to 90, who are experienced in the art of Smiling.

We want men who have learned the value of a Smile not only when everything goes along smoothly but those who have learned to Smile when everything goes dead wrong and when it seems as though nothing on earth is worth while.

That's the kind of Smilers we want.

We want TRAINED Smilers. We want habitual Smilers — confirmed Smilers, Smilers that have the knack of giving away Smiles. We want Smilers who know how to produce Smiles on the faces of people where no Smiles ever played before.

We don't care anything about where you come from or what your business is or how many Ancestors you may have had. You must have the business of Smiling absolutely mastered. And we don't want Smilers who have learned to Smile but a part of the day or on "set" occasions.

We want the Chronic Smilers. We have a job for you. We ask for One Thousand. We really want every one that we can get. We ask for MEN Smilers. But we actually want just as many WOMEN Smilers.

When do we want them? Now. Where do we want them? Everywhere. Who wants them? Everybody. What for? To make this world the best possible world in which to live.

APPLY — at your own Home or Living Place, your Office, or on the Street — wherever your Face takes you. But keep your SMILE with you. For without it — none need apply.

Books

FIND out what Books your Friend reads and you'll know what manner of man or woman you have for a Friend. Books contain the wisdom — as well as the foolishness of the ages. The greatest thoughts, the deepest experiences, the results of the most profound and prolonged experiments, are all embalmed in books.

Grow useful from Books.

The Character of a man is shown by the Books he selects. The Character of a Nation is largely determined by the Books that its men and women read. The wealth of the world is in its Books, not in its Gold and Silver and precious Stones and Structures and Lands.

Grow useful from Books.

Good books are real. They are cross sections of life. They tell the truth and conceal nothing. You take or leave what such a book teaches. You know, without asking, its true value. You think, act, walk, work — live with it. For the time you are of it — a part. You live over the thought that the writer lived. Though long years in his grave — again he breathes, and warmth is in his blood again. How marvelous is a Book!

Grow useful from Books.

Good Books make sympathy a world trait. Progress is but the accumulation of Book power. With books gone the world would rot away. Good Books will put Poetry and Music into your smallest efforts.

Grow useful from Books.

The world's greatest doers have been the world's greatest readers, "Read again," said Napoleon to an officer on board the ship that was taking him into exile forever, "read again the poets; devour Ossian. Poets lift up the soul, and give to man a collossal greatness."

Grow useful from Books.

Read Good Books regularly and systematically. Learn Books. Love Books. LIVE Books.

Radiate

THE most useful body in the heavens is the Sun. It keeps the world out of continual darkness. It Radiates its greatest gift — light. Also it Radiates its heat — keeps this old Earth warm. Take a lesson from the Sun —

Radiate you Influence.

Make it worth Radiating. Radiate it to your Friends. Radiate it to your Office Helpers. Radiate it in your Public Position. Radiate it through your own approval, and take to heart the responsibility that gives you the chance to make your Influence.

Radiate your Smiles.

For Smiles and Chew are the greatest stimulators in the world. You don't have to speak to Radiate Smiles and Cheer. They shoot their rays of warmth and healing and encouragement from the very lines of your Face and the very movements of your body.

Radiate your Knowledge.

Do it to a high purpose. Knowledge kept is of no value whatever. The only Knowledge worth having is what you give away. What Knowledge you get, Radiate.

Radiate your Money.

Earn it honestly and well Then Radiate it to useful ends. Divide it with the faithful workers who helped you make it. Money is the most useless thing in itself. Its total value lies in what it Radiates in hopeful enterprises and noble works.

Radiate your Success.

There is nothing so stimulating, to a real Winner as to hand out the secrets and formulas of Success that he has learned. Nature works in rotation. So does a man's Success. What is yours today is the other fellow's tomorrow. Your service is to keep the law — to Radiate today what came to you yesterday. For the whole rule of life and Success is to Radiate — To Radiate.

Courtesy

TO SOME Courtesy may seem a Lost Art, little worth bringing back. But it is not. Courtesy is one of the Old Time Arts that dies only with the Man or the Business. For the rise of many a Man and Business has started with it.

Take time to be Courteous.

Emerson once wrote: "Give a boy address and accomplishments, and you give him the mastery of Palaces and Fortunes wherever he goes." Courtesy is of more value to a man than a thousand letters of written recommendations. Courtesy is an asset of more power than Money or Influence.

Take time to be Courteous.

A few years ago, a young man by the name of Wallace stood behind a Railroad office window in Oil City, Pennsylvania, as a Ticket Agent. But he didn't stay there ALL the time. When he saw a chance to render a Courteous favor by delivering tickets direct to a customer, he delivered the tickets. Also, he sought out new ways of giving service. Business grew. A bigger

job came after him. Then a bigger one. Today, still a young man, he is General Passenger Agent for the entire Erie Railroad. He may be its President someday. He owes his career to Courtesy.

Take time to be Courteous.

Courtesy lightens the burdens of toil. Courtesy demands respect. Courtesy is a little brother to Opportunity and follows her around through the hours of the busy day. Courtesy always leads a man higher up.

Take time to be Courteous.

The Courteous Office Boy, the Courteous Clerk, the Courteous Stenographer, the Courteous Manager, the Courteous Leader at heavy tasks — whoever heard of such a one not growing, not climbing into greater things? Think over these truths. For it is tremendously worth while to —

Take time to be Courteous.

Aim

HAVE a definite purpose — Aim. The secret of all Winning is the unyielding fight toward a definite Ideal or Plan. A man with a set Aim and the courage to follow in its path cannot Fail. In feet, what you Aim to be, you already are — potentially.

Have a definite purpose — Aim.

The first efforts of John Keats were laughed to scorn by his critics, but he paid no attention to them, for he was certain of his ability and hardly was the ink on their criticisms dry before he handed them his marvelous poem Endymion. "I was never afraid of failure," said he, "for I would sooner fail than not be among the greatest." Keats was but twenty-six years of age when he died — a mere boy! But he had a world fame — he had achieved his Aim.

Have a definite purpose — Aim.

Washington lost more battles than he won. But his Aim for Independence was achieved. People marvel at the election to the Presidency of Woodrow Wilson — a Schoolmaster. But those who know the man, know that he has been preparing for this exalted office for a quarter of a century — not Aiming at the Office merely — but the ability to FILL it. His Aim was to merit the Task — not the Honor alone.

Have a definite purpose — Aim.

There are no "Lucky Dogs." Winners are just the Workers with an Aim — that's all. The Successful business men of every city — the largest number of them — had nothing to begin with but a single Aim. What is their story now? The magnificent blocks, and great enterprises that make each city what it is. Have you an Aim? You only need ONE big central Aim. Get it without delay. Then follow it consistently and courageously. For it is better to Aim at one great task and complete it acceptably and with Honor, than to split your Aims into a dozen different Aims and win in none.

Have a definite purpose — Aim.

Thanks

THE Thank habit is one of the best habits that you can form. Think for a moment. Did you ever regret a "Thank you," received from anybody? Did it ever make you feel mean, dissatisfied, out of sorts? Has it ever brought to you a feeling of remorse for service rendered? Alright, then —

Get the Thank habit.

It is not necessary to express in mere words at all times your feeling of Thankfulness. Once get the habit thoroughly and you will LIVE it unconsciously. Thankful men and women show in their very eyes and attitude that they have the habit. It's the most "showy" quality possible. It's contagious, too.

Get the Thank habit.

You meet a gruff, inhuman being. He performs some service as though he were a sort of mechanical device. You Thank him. He at once becomes Human! Thankfulness acts like a powerful stimulant both on yourself and upon other people. It transforms. All days are fine days, all people are square people, all happenings are for the best to the one who has thoroughly mastered the "Thank Habit."

Get the Thank habit.

Get it by always acknowledging a service with a Thank you. If your Clerk, or Waiter, or Secretary, or Partner, or Friend does a service — no matter how small — hand over the Thanks — freely, with a broad, healthy Smile. It's a great investment. The Dividends simply roll back to you.

Get the Thank habit.

Reserve

REAL Strength does not show its full force on all occasions. Often it only pokes its head out. Real Strength has Reserve power. The strongest part of great buildings is under ground — in rock and steel and mortar — where eyes cannot see. Success Power is in the Reserve. Reserve is the law of Nature and of Life. When the Reserve is gone, all is gone. The greatest battles are won with Reserve forces; Banks are kept steady and safe by their Reserve funds; Business goes on, healthy and vigorous because of its Reserve capital. The character of a man or woman — YOUR character — is kept from being swept easily into oblivion, through the safe Reserve that you lock securely away in the shape of stores of Honor, Courage, Faith, Backbone — all ready for emergencies.

Success Power is in the Reserve.

Reserve is what keeps the Smile from fading into the frown. Reserve is what makes possible the next trial after the last one failed.

Success Power is in the Reserve.

The Human failure begins by being too proud to work for six dollars a week. The Human Success is ANXIOUS and glad of the chance to work for three dollars a week at the start. For Reserve is also the knowledge of sure future — concealed from the general view, yet known to the individual.

Success Power is in the Reserve.

Do every detail of your day's work as though it was to be viewed by a Master eye. Make every job a great job. Put Dignity and Joy and

Enthusiasm into everything attempted, forgetting not for the shortest minute that —

Success Power is in the Reserve.

To Stenographers

SOMEWHERE in every busy city is a Stenographer that is Wanted. Young, neat, of good family, educated, she clicks away at her type keys with evenness and with care.

Accurate, attentive, enthusiastic, she works through the hours with speed in her work and joy in her heart, and all backed by a good level head.

This young lady uses her Brains as well as her Fingers. She is making good. She would make good anywhere. That is why she is Wanted today by scores of Business Men. She takes an interest not only in her own work at hand but in the work of her Employer. She constantly seeks for new chances to help and to grow. Her Character is felt in the office and it radiates its influence of strength wherever she goes and in whatever she does.

She is not the Girl-here-today, Girl-there-tomorrow sort. That is another reason why she is Wanted by dozens of other Concerns. Prompt at her duties in the morning, she has no concern for the Clock at night. Courteous, cheerful, thoughtful of the interests of others, she demands respect — and gets it.

Of the Gum chewing, Candy eating, Vanity box, office Cult she is not a part. Work to her is a Business and a Training. Also, it's a Development that she guards and takes pride in. She sees Visions and Value and Personal Growth that no pay envelop could possibly hold.

As stated, this young lady is Wanted — Wanted badly. Every Business house in every city is in imperative need of her. Her services are Wanted TODAY! She will need no further qualifications than those named as already having. But will she kindly — without fail — call TODAY? She may call at any Business house in any city for she is Wanted by them ALL.

Point-Of-View

HOURLY thousands of human wrecks topple heedlessly over the Niagara of a Ragged Point-Of-View, and strew the Rapids of Failure into a pitiful sight. The reason? Rudder out of Setting!

Set YOUR Rudder before Sailing.

The boy in School who has as his end but the fitting of his Lesson to the mere Classroom hour, the Clerk who but dreams of his day as done with the end of his eight hours, the man who measures his Success by the weight of his Dollars — these are but illustrations of the Point-Of-View in Life — turned backward — out of Kink. There is but one way to reach the real Port of real Success and that is to —

Set YOUR Rudder before Sailing.

For a Point-Of-View is just plain Purpose. And there is just one kind of Purpose worth any man's or woman's Salt — the Purpose that tends to some USEFUL end.

Set YOUR Rudder before Sailing.

If you start this day with a healthy Point-Of-View, you will end it a happier, healthier, broader, bigger person. How wonderful, too, the individual effect that a high, square Point-of-View has, not upon yourself alone but on your whole environment. In fact, how it makes

Environment!

Set YOUR Rudder before Sailing.

Get the right Point-Of-View upon Life. Then it will permeate your Work — make rich the lives of your Friends and your Achievements, bringing at the same time to you a rounded Success. Search out the proper Point-of-View for each task DAILY. In other words —

Set YOUR Rudder before Sailing.

Wait

LEARN to Wait.

Not idly, but with the spirit of Busyness in your system working itself out into some useful Endeavor. For to know HOW to Wait is to master one of the greatest secrets of Success.

Learn to Wait.

The parents of Balzac were wealthy. The son at the age of twenty announced his determination to become an Author. "But," urged his Father, "do you not know that in literature a man must be either king or hodman?" "Very well," replied the young man, "I'll be king!" He was, therefore, abandoned to a rude garret, where for ten years he labored against the fiercest poverty and obstacles. But his Waiting and Work won. Balzac's name will remain among the greatest in the literature of all time.

Learn to Wait.

To Wait, intelligently, is ability in itself of the rarest sort. For it is a quality imbedded in Fortitude, Self Mastery and Will.

Learn to Wait.

You hold a humble position. You are restless. You see others of less ability and brains passing you. Wait. The prizes of life seem to you to be unevenly distributed. Wait. The click and glare of Gold and Silver play songs to your senses. But Wait. Do more than you are paid for in real work and conscientious Effort. Conquer the Trifles. Reap the respect of your Superiors. Wait. And your rise to power shall be as the rise to power of the men and women who have made this world what it is.

Learn to Wait.

Stomachs

THE Stomach is the Firebox of the Body. Its simple construction, patterned by a Supreme Master, is imitated by the human makers of the greatest Engines in the world — Engines that have knit Civilization and populated Nations.

Respect your Stomach.

Every human Stomach is from the same mould. But never has there been born a human being that took care of his Stomach in quite the same way. In real importance, greater than any other organ of the human Body, it is least respected — it is most neglected.

Respect your Stomach.

For your Stomach is your Success. Nothing can replace a ruined Stomach. Think seriously of this as you burn its walls with the beautifully colored contents of dainty Glasses. Think of this when you hurriedly throw into its marvelous pocket, ill selected and quickly masticated Food. Think of this as you neglect its call for regular Fuel and regular Care. Think of this when it begs for Rest.

Respect your Stomach.

No Stomach ever turned Traitor to a good Care- taker. A companionable Stomach will work wonders for its Master. It will build Power for scores of years. It will knit Strength and Elasticity into Bones and Muscles. It will create unfailing Nerve Centers. It will pump a great Heart. It will give an iron Will and a masterful Brain.

Kind Stomachs are more than Coronets, and simple care to them, than Norman Blood.

Respect your Stomach.

Morning, Noon and Night — and between times —

Respect your Stomach.

Today

THIS is the most important day in the history of the world. Because it is the Latest Day — and the only Day of its kind that shall ever dawn again.

There is no Tomorrow — Today.

Worry shall have no part of this Day. Disappointment, Fear, Envy, Bitterness, Regret, Anger, Selfishness, and their like — they are of the Past a part. They must have naught of standing or of voice in this Day. For, as already said, THIS Day shall never come around again. Its reception must be Royal and the works in its twenty-four hours must be performed with serious consideration and under the bearing of Responsibility and Appreciation.

There is no Tomorrow — Today.

Your Smile Today will be worth the millions in the Tomorrow. Your Efforts, your Deeds, your Courtesies, your Words, your written Thoughts, your ALL, will count for more Today than all your mapped out plans of twenty years to come.

There is no Tomorrow — Today.

What odds if your ancestors were Monkeys a few years back — so you are a Man Today! Whether or no you shall be the Great man or woman ten years from Today shall depend on what manner of acting man or woman you are Today. There are no accidents of Destiny. The Big Thing to be is the Little Thing to do — Today.

There is no Tomorrow — Today.

Manners

IT is inferred that Manners make the Man. No — the Man makes the Manners. For Manners are the Man. And they point the path of Interpretation to a Character as surely as does the weather-vane tell exactly the direction of the wind.

Be your Best Self always.

You enter a car, an office, a home, pace a street. People — your like and image — you meet everywhere. Your Manners in their presence mark your standing and your own enjoyment. Your smile, your graciousness, your courtesy, change the gruff attitude of a clerk or the cold reception of the one you face whether it be for your profit or his.

Be your Best Self always.

"Sir," once said Dr. Johnson, "a man has no more right to say a rude thing to another than to knock him down." The man or woman of Manners is the person of consideration and tact. And nothing but the inbred quality of Manner is genuine. For money or social standing or quick achievement cannot give it.

Be your Best Self always.

Now, Manners are a possession most enviable. Few are born without the possibility of them. A large number who have them hidden away somewhere use them not. To find them out and put them to use and to habit is an event much to be heralded. A better day than this to start could not be found. How about polishing them up at home? How about carrying them as you do your grip or morning paper to your office? How about investing them, as sure dividend bringers, in your office helpers and day associates — from the humblest to the greatest? You can do so if you decide as a settled thing to —

Be your Best Self always.

Relax

ACHIEVEMENT is the result of the proper co-ordination between Work and Rest. Were it not for its regular fraction-of-a-second Rest between each throb, the Heart would soon pump itself out.

Relaxation is Energy Stored Up.

Go into any Business Office. Hunt out the man whose work seems to be going on with Smoothness and with the least Friction. Study him carefully — for he is sure to be the Boss himself. Having no time for foolish dreams and useless details, yet such a man is never too busy to Listen and to Learn — and Relax. He makes every effort Count — by periodic Resting.

Relaxation is Energy Stored Up.

There is to Relaxation a quiet, cumulative power that is sure to hold you in good stead if ever Panic or Disorder come near. For it is at such times that every ounce of energy and resource is demanded.

Relaxation is Energy Stored Up.

Relax as you Work. Think as you Go. Reflect upon the Improvement of everything you Do. All things can wait upon a man building up and fortifying his own Soul and his own Character. Invest in Relaxation.

Self-Control

SELF-CONTROL is simply manly Courage fully fit- ready to act calmly in Emergency. It's the Man at the helm in complete Power. Also, Self-Control is the Man Self-Happy because Self-Bossed.

You can Be what you Will, if you Will to Be.

Pot the intricate Forces of the Brain cluster about each other seeking a Leader. And the Man-power steps out and takes command. First of all, you are what you are. Rude hands never shaped you. Divinity formed you in the raw. Then Divinity must shape you into the Strong. Self-Control is the cornerstone of Divinity.

You can Be what you Will, if you Will to Be.

Rule your own Self and you immediately find yourself in the center of things, for you draw others your way. The great Shop with its thousands of wheels, belts, bolts and screws, all working in the smoothest unison, grips the admiration as its marvelous Power Plant, human-like in perfect Self-Control, produces its completed Machines. But greater are you in your Human Shop, while under absolute Self-Control, you turn out Deeds worthy and un-ending.

You can Be what you Will, if you Will to Be.

Self-Control must needs be made up of Patience, the ability to keep Still when you feel like Talking right out, and the iron holding down of your own Self for the sake of the Bigger Hours. No man ever won anything with- out first winning Himself. You are a strong Human bundle of Passion, Red Pepper — and Power. Your Mixing of these things in wise proportion and mastering them will mould you into a sure Success. Try, for —

You can Be what you Will, if you Will to Be.

Influence

JUST as soon as you begin to Think or Do something, you begin to have Influence. Influence is something you can't keep at home. And when it gets away from you, you can never call it back.

Your Influence makes you Something of Somebody else.

Influence has no boundaries. Once started, though it may seem ever so trifling, yet it may have as its destination the farthermost corners of the Earth. If you would get a conception of Power, realize the Influence of a Strong Man.

It is well to remember that what you have that you can't help but give away is your Influence.

Bear in mind that your Influence is never wholly absorbed, nor does it disappear into Nothingness. It Counts again and again. Influence has no end.

The three greatest objects in life — Friends, Happiness, Success — are each dependent upon proper Influence. So it is good to know that even the humblest person is, after all, master of his own Influence. He can send it out to scatter Sunshine or Shadows. It's his Choice.

A man's greatest Responsibility in this world lies in the way he acquires and gives out — his Influence.

Your Influence today is sure to have a tremendous bearing upon the total work of the world. Your Influence upon other people and the Influence of other people upon you is sure to become a Force and a Factor in the complete work of your day and theirs.

See that your Influence is kept true and wholesome and it will return to refresh you, again and again.

Face It

SOME people fancy that to Dodge some work that they ought to do is about the easiest possible thing to do. The truth is, however, it is always easier to walk right up to your work and — Face It.

No one but laggards dig up excuses for Dodging what they should Face.

It is unfortunate that the most costly lessons are many times learned late in life. The greatest reason for this is our timidity and cowardice in Facing every problem just as soon as it Faces us. Many a man has evaded a problem in his youth that he could easily have Solved at that time and then gone on, but which he refused to grapple with until compelled to Face It late in life under cover of the bitterest pangs of sorrow and remorse.

It takes greater courage to Decide to do a thing than it does to Do the thing.

Have you a particularly difficult piece of Work to do today? Face It. Have you an Enemy? Face him — and make him your Friend. You feel yourself capable of more important work than you are now doing? Face the new Work, and decide to Master it. Whatever your Problem, Face It — with Courage and without Fear, and with the Calmness that comes to a man when he decides to go ahead according to his Conscience.

Sidestep — Dodge, from nothing. If a thing is worth working out, Face It and Finish it.

Poise

POISE is a large phase of Success already worked out. For there can be little of Success without Poise. Poise is keeping your head when everybody else loses theirs.

Poise is Power — square jawed and firm set.

When Blame all seems to come your way; when the fingers of Fault-finders all seem centered in front of your face; when Failure after Failure files into your door; when former Friends form into foes; when Clouds creep onward, black and threatening — then's the time for

Poise!

Then's the time to face the Crowd and cut the air with your command of Confidence and — Poise.

The Cool heads are the Battle winners.

And you who are ruling and conserving through the art of Poise, you are preserving Peace by being prepared for War.

The Strong Man always Listens — and Thinks. In such an attitude he can consider and weigh with Justice and rare Freedom the most puzzling problems. Poise to such a man is like a Bank full of funds.

Poise put into your Character will balance and proportion it — make it fit and formidable.

How many times you have seen the Man of Action at his desk, calm and collected — with plenty of time for anything important — while about him is confusion and an atmosphere of importance that is, after all, charged with very little importance.

Study out and apply to yourself — Poise. Poise starts when you begin to eliminate Fear and Disorder.

Capacity

YOUR Capacity is the stored up Power that you have available for your Everyday Doing as well as for the various Emergencies of your Life. Also, Capacity is the Valuation chalked up as your Real Assets which you and you alone know as your own.

Capacity is Possibility.

The very knowledge that you possess Capacity is in itself an inspiration most extraordinary. It enables you to tread your way bravely and under cover of Smiles with Sunshine streaming into every corner of your Heart. For you to know that you have Capacity to go through a piece of work or to the accomplishment of a certain Purpose or Ideal is to you more than Wealth.

Capacity is Possibility.

Many a man has turned away from his employ many a worker whose Capacity he took no time to investigate, but which later had to be reckoned with in Competition. When the late Marshall Field discovered unusual Capacity in a worker, he recognized it and later joined it to his business in the shape of a Partner.

Capacity is Possibility.

Study yourself as you would a masterful piece of machinery, for you are the most wonderful Handiwork that has ever been put together. Each day should find you more familiar with your Abilities and Capacity than the day before. Your latent and undiscovered or unrealized Capacity may now be holding you into Mediocrity. Ask yourself if this is true. Find out what your Capacity suggests and you can be about what you determine to be.

Things to Do

THE people who get the most done — and still seem to have the most time on their hands for other things — are the ones who go at their work from a carefully mapped out plan. For in the end, it's the one who conserves and uses to its full, the 24 hours of Time at his command, that Leads and Rules.

The Successful are they that See and Do — the Unsuccessful are they that See — and do not Do.

Having Things To Do — and doing them according to Plan has produced sufficient Romance in the Business of the World, which if written out, would remain undying in its inspiration to succeeding generations.

A single illustration here. Hugh Chalmers, but a few years ago Office Boy, then Salesman, then Sales Manager, then Vice-President and General Manager, of the National Cash Register Company — now President of a Concern he himself organized and doing business into the millions! Each night Mr. Chalmers' Secretary writes out on a little slip the ten most important Things To Do for the next Day.

Time used in Thinking out things the night before or at the beginning of each day and putting them into logical order for Action is Time invested in advance.

Victor Hugo says: "He who every morning plans the transactions of the day and follows out the plan, carries a thread that will guide him through the labyrinth of the most busy life. The orderly arrangement of his time is like a ray of light which darts itself through all his operations."

Ancestors

ARE you one of those people who like to putter away valuable time figuring out just how you stand as to Ancestors? The fact is, your Ancestors were what YOU are. Some of the best and worst that have gone before you is now somewhere in you.

The wisest thing you can do is to discover the most useful qualities of your Ancestry inside yourself, and begin to weave — from where it left off — greater and bigger things.

Ancestry stock goes up every time you do your work better Today than Yesterday.

A story is told of Ney, one of Napoleon's famous Marshals. At a banquet during the Russian campaign, a brilliant woman had been telling Ney of her wonderful

Ancestry, when suddenly she questioned: "By the way, Marshal Ney, who were YOUR Ancestors?" "Madam," answered Ney, "I, myself, am an Ancestor!"

After all, the task of being an Ancestor is mighty serious business. It is enough to put us all on our mettle and make us work to force the Red Blood into our Arteries.

In just the proportion that men and women render Service in this world do they forget their own selfish interests and begin to plan out and deal in "the Futures" of their Race. The man who will but get this truth imbedded into his system cannot fail to be a better Clerk, Lawyer, Business Man, Father — or Citizen. And no woman can take this idea to heart without putting Luster to the important duties of her life.

Ancestors? Why, we are ALL Ancestors!

Tomorrow

TO the fellow who never accomplished anything Tomorrow is what happened yesterday, but which he seeks to make happen today.

The thing put off until Tomorrow is rarely done Today.

The great Task FINISHED is always the task done Today, while yet there is Time, while yet there is inclination, while yet there is life and health — while yet there is Chance.

The thing put off until Tomorrow is rarely done Today.

Some of the biggest things ever accomplished were done in a day. Napoleon was banished to a living Hell — on a lonely rock with armed watchers hedged about him — for the simple reason that Blucher decided to do his part with Wellington without any courting with Tomorrow. Tomorrow for Grouchy meant Defeat for Napoleon for Blucher, "made good" Today.

The thing put off until Tomorrow is rarely done Today.

It may be easier to do things Tomorrow than Today, but if you take the Chance, the one best bet is that they won't get done. Money earned Today represents Dividends for you Tomorrow. Work entered into and done Today renders back Ease and Satisfaction Tomorrow. Records made Today, inspire and lead great armies of fighters Tomorrow. But —

The thing put off until Tomorrow is rarely done Today.

The Liar

LYING is the most despicable of all Crimes. The liar is the King of Criminals. The last clean spot in a man's raiment turns Crimson when he takes up the Business of Lying.

Truth is the Highest Thing a man can keep.

The Heart of an honest man melts away almost unto Death in the presence of the Liar. The very mercy of a kind God blushes with bowed head in Sadness at the sight and sound of the man who plies his Lies. Scorned by Society, the very Soul of the liar revolts at the carrying about of Bones and Flesh so vile.

Truth is the Highest Thing a man can keep.

Recently a young man, large of Mind and Future, left his employment with a lie upon his lips. Coming into the seething whirl of the Great New York he sought his former friends. Immediately he began to hand out a stock of Lies. More abominably than any abandoned thief he slyly exchanged his lies for Favors and for Gold. Then nervously yet quietly sneaking away under cover of his Lies, his Soul naked of Honor and Character, he sought refuge under his own-made Tent of Lies. There Self-convicted he now awaits Judgment.

Truth is the Highest Thing a man can keep.

Mark Twain spoke more than humor when he said: "When in doubt, speak the Truth." Even the Devil hates a Liar — one of his own children. And Nature itself closes its eyes in shame as the Liar passes by.

Truth is the Highest Thing a man can keep.

You — Young Man, Young Woman, Business Builder, Doer of Things — whoever you are, and in whatever groove you work your way — listen! Starve — die, rather than Lie. Flee from the presence of a lie as from the Plague. Grasp the clean, strong hand of Truth and follow in its path through the livelong hours of every single passing day. Remembering that —

Truth is the Highest Thing a man can keep.

Forward

THIS is a talk to Women. Both Unmarried and Married. The theme insures Happiness and Inspiration. It has to do with Advancement. Here it is —

Keep Step.

Keep Step with The Man. For he has mostly secured his Steps to something better from you. Behind the Greatness and Work of every man there has always been the name of some noble woman who was greater than the Deed or Work performed by The Man. The world will always bow its head in reverence at the naming of the Mothers and Wives of the Makers of History.

Keep Step.

The young fellow whose name you hope to link to yours — he is taking his "cue" these days from you. You, who already have him with you — how about it? Is he getting his Steps from you? And are you Keeping Step? If not, start now to —

Keep Step.

A man is as great as the Woman who loves him — makes and wants him to be. A great Man can never be greater than a great woman who helps make him great. Your Power is his. But if you give no Power, his clipped wings make him walk sadly alone. His fight then may become one against the Inevitable.

Keep Step.

As he Learns — you Learn. As he Climbs — you Climb. As he Fights — you Fight. As he Wins — you Win. As long as this world lasts, you, who sometimes think yourself "just a woman" will lead and rule. It's your Kingdom, after all. But in the Home, in Business, and before the eyes of people in Public, this must be your love and your life — with The Man —

Keep Step.

Ragged Edges

BACK of all the tragedy of Failure there is always the tragic truth of Neglect and Slight — edges left ragged and incomplete.

Finish up as you Go.

A few years ago a young man in a Western College got restless and discouraged. He wanted to leave his course unfinished. He sought the advice of a successful man and this was the advice: "Stick it out. Finish Something. There are too many men now with Ragged Edges crowding the ranks." The young man Finished his College course with honors. Today he is a Leader and a Success.

Finish up as you Go.

Many a man stops work with the clock. He leaves his day's work with Ragged Edges. He is the man who starts his days with Ragged Edges, and finally rounds out an incomplete life.

Finish up as you Go.

There is a satisfaction and a feeling of latent Strength in the breast of a man who Starts a thing — and Finishes it. You will find this true if you do it. The most important task is always the task at hand. Complete it. Make it stand square and clean when you leave it. Look it over. Be sure no Ragged Edges remain.

Finish up as you Go.

Make Thoroughness one of your Masters. Searchingly note the trifles. Get them together and know them. For out of them comes — Perfection.

Finish up as you Go.

Bystanders

IN life you are either on the Side Lines or else in the Game. If you are on the Side Lines you are merely watching. You are inactive. You are contributing to your personal pleasure. If you are in the Game you are playing hard, you are getting pleasure and you are rendering Service.

You will always get more pleasure out of the Game if you are a Player instead of a Bystander.

All along the streets of any town or city are lined the Bystanders. Inside the Stores and Offices and Factories are housed the Workers. The Workers are the ones who support the Bystanders.

Let no man do for you what you ought to do for Yourself.

To be the mere title-holder of a Job counts for little. You must be the Job in every sense of the word or else you may be classed with the Bystanders.

The worst thing about the Bystander is that he Contributes neither to himself nor other people — he is a

Blank.

The surest law in the world is the Law of Compensation. Its Justice works continually. If you do a Service you get back a Service. If you do Nothing you get back Nothing. Mere existence is not Living.

Into your twenty-four hours put Work and Play and Rest, but at no time be a Bystander.

Tongues.

ONE of the most difficult things in this world to get control of is the human Tongue. Kipling never said anything truer than when he wrote that "Man may hold most any post if he'll only hold his Tongue."

Before you set your Tongue to action get it under perfect Control.

A single Tongue can do more harm in the world than a Battalion of Soldiers. For Soldiers can kill but Bodies while the Tongue can kill Reputations and Characters. It is too bad that we have no laws to curb Tongues. Shakespeare powerfully pictured in the character of Iago the terrible consequences following in the path of an evil Tongue. Iago not only destroyed the Reputation and pure Character of Desdemona, but he finally, through Othello, killed her body.

Compel your Tongue to speak Helpful Messages or else keep it still.

Make it a rule of your life to use your Tongue for high purposes alone. Resolve to speak in no way of any man or woman unless you can speak of the good qualities of that man or woman. No one ever gained Happiness out of injuring the Feelings or Character of someone else. No one ever failed to get Happiness by speaking well of other people.

The Golden Rule applied to the Tongue comprises one of the real Golden Rules of Conduct.

The "George" Habit

IF you only realized how much you miss in Pleasure, Growth and increased Power every time you push Responsibility upon someone else, you would never again let a chance pass to do what comes to, you to do.

Once for all, break the "Let George Do It" habit. When a task steps up before you — take hold of it and do it Yourself.

In every community — in this community — there are always big, ready, generous, willing people quick to respond to any call for Service at the moment someone else shirks. They are the "Georges." And if you will let them perform your work, they will do it. But when they do — you move Backward. YOU — be a "George."

Work that should be done by Yourself is never done so well when shifted to someone else.

You are either a Do or a Let Do. It is a personal matter of Success or Failure as to which you are.

The "Let George Do It" folks are easily spotted. They line the sidewalks of every busy street. They do the "easy" jobs in the Stores and Factories. They are the fellows that board at Jails and Alms Houses and keep the Lawyers busy. They are the men and women that are "too busy" to do what is asked and required of them to do.

Don't "Let George Do It." Do it YOURSELF.

Friends

FRIENDS are essentials. Just as air and food and clothing are essentials. For is not he who has no Friends lacking and lonely and useless? Who ever heard of a useless man having Friends? Like attracts like. No one ever secured a Friend without first vibrating the Friend spirit within himself.

To get a Friend you must be a Friend.

The Friend art is a Heart art — all else cheapens it. He to whom we talk and confide and trust is but another of us transplanted where courage and cheer and kindness is ever alert. We go to our Friend and he lifts us up and we feel him coming back to his own again — in ourselves.

A Friend is a mutual partner with whom we need no signed agreements.

It is said of Carlyle and Tennyson that they would at for hours together without the passing of a word and then separate. And both inspired and uplifted because of the meeting! To reach the priceless treasure veins of a Friend it is necessary to go deep. In the presence of real Friends a sort of Divinity hovers.

Back of the knowledge that you have a Friend is the secret of your ability to press on and win at your plans.

The glory of Friend joy depends not in numbers. Have but one real Friend — and it is enough! The one that will not refuse to understand you, or protect you, but that through the solid and harsh hour of test, will gladly be the other half of the fight with you.

He is your Friend who brings out of you the best of which you are capable.

You and your Friend plan no Parades. You are as

you are. The sincerity of Service leads you on — makes each day as certain of Success as though it had already been completed and handed to you. If you are in doubt as to what you ought to be in the world, set your- self to the task of making of yourself a great Friend. Remembering that —

A lifetime is all too short in which to be a Friend and get Friends.

Play

TO you who early learn the value of Play applied to your life, and to you who learn just when to apply it, there is opened a road, both wide and short into the town of Peace, Power and Plenty.

Play.

Play stretches the Muscles, rests and soothes the Nerves, stirs the Blood and Clears the Brain. Play Stays the Hand of Age and transplants Youth all along through the advancing Years.

Play.

Play lifts the Burdens from people's shoulders — Smoothes out the Wrinkles from their Faces and starts Smiles and Joy anew.

Play.

Play is a Strangler of Worry, an Enemy of Ill-Health and a mighty Force in the Creating of Clean, Strong Thinking. Play is Insurance against Failure.

Play.

Play at outdoor Sports. Play at your Books. Play with your "kiddies" if you have them, and with other people's "kiddies" if you have none yourself. Play before you start your day and Play at its Close. And occasionally "skip" a day that you may also Play.

Play.

Play hard when you do Play. But never Play when you Work and never Work when you Play. Neither make Play out of Work nor Work out of Play.

Your Mother

THE sweetest word in the Language of Languages is that of — Mother. There is in each letter of this word a wealth of music so Divine — there are vibrating chords of Love so Angelic — that the whole world often pays Homage to Mothers whom it honors.

Nancy Hanks — the Mother of Lincoln; Frances

Willard and Jane Addams — Mothers to the Motherless; Queen Victoria — the Mother of a Nation of Mothers.

You — whoever you are — your greatest Asset is your Mother. You — bankrupt, discouraged, failure-riddled, hope-wasted, heart-wrenched, self-estranged — there remains still a Day, glorious in Sunsets for you if you will but get back again, in Thought, or Heart, or Person — to your Mother.

The most wonderful Event in the History of the World was when the first Woman became — a Mother. Human Life has become a beautiful thing because the world has had its Mothers.

The greatest Characters in every community are the Mothers. The greatest community is that which honors its Mothers most. The greatest men in any community are those who render the highest tribute to Motherhood.

No one ever has Surpassed or ever will Surpass the achievement of a Woman when she becomes a Mother.

When did you last write to your Mother? If she has gone from you, how often do you think of her? Do you realize that all you are or ever hope to be, started back into the years when your Mother, her whole being pulsating with Pride, held you tight, and with eyes lustred and watered with Love, watched your very Breath, and kept pace, over the hours, with your faintest Heart Throbs? Think of how, all through those days she wrapped you in her Unselfishness and her Sacrifices.

The measure of your Success will be the degree of Honor you pay to your Mother and to Motherhood.

How many indelicate stories would you tell if your Mother could always be present? How many mean and unjust affairs would you bring to pass if you had the eyes of your Mother looking on? Never mind about the "Apron Strings." There always comes a time when there are no "Apron Strings" to be tied to. And then you will long for them to come back.

If ever Failure begins to press; if ever Friends begin to fade away; if ever the grand figure of your Will shall begin to bow its Power — do this — think of your Mother and live up to her ideals of you.

Kiss your Mother as you go into the fight of this day. And at its close fill her furrowed forehead with your Smiles. Ease her Cares. Write to her though business go to Smash. Go and see her often though it takes you across the Globe. Let her Living Presence keep you Courageous. And if she has gone from you let her Memory Guide and Inspire you as once you Guided and Inspired her Faith.

Salt

STIR up your Salt.

For Salt — translated into terms of moral use — is the stuff that seasons and balances one's work — keeps it from swaying into mediocrity, commonness and nothingness — it's Grit, Courage, Backbone, refined to the crystal degree. That's Salt!

Stir up your Salt.

A man without Salt in his system is about as active a thing as a watch without works. Neither one goes.

Stir up your Salt.

The blood and body of a man is saturated with Salt. When a man's Salt runs out the man runs out.

Stir up your Salt.

Salt is the thing that savors Mankind.

Stir up your Salt.

You are worth your Salt if you have worth to add to your Salt. Salt has no value alone. Salt is a partner ingredient. It's a complement to what you already have to mix with it.

Stir up your Salt.

Salt is at once the commonest and rarest thing in all the world. It's nowhere — yet almost everywhere. But it's yours to take and use. Salt in your work is evenness of Effort, stolidness of Purpose and assuredness of Faith in Results — Hope for better things — Courage for bigger tasks. As you work through the minutes and the hours, keep it firmly in mind that Success must needs have its share of Salt.

Stir up your Salt.

Habit

HABIT is a fixed series of acts. Do a thing once and Tracks are marked. Do a thing twice and a Route is mapped. Do a thing thrice and a Path is blazed.

Do the Right thing over and over again.

Prom the unconscious wink of the eye to the smooth, unnoticed movements of a million worlds, the law of Habit relentlessly rules its course. All life is but a set of Habits.

Do the Right thing over and over again.

The Pennies saved today make the Nickels in the bank tomorrow. The Nickels in the bank tomorrow spell the Dollars in the bank next year. The Dollars saved, crystallize into the Fortune after the years! Habit either makes or breaks — either leads you up or drags you down.

Do the Right thing over and over again.

If you are Prompt today you will want to be Prompt tomorrow. If you are Square once you will surely seek to be Square again. The fight for a thing Worth While right now cannot help but ease the fight for the thing Worth While later on. It is the law of Habit. And Habit creeps on from the minutest Action repeated over and over again.

Do the Right thing over and over again.

Grow Great off of Habit! There is no other way. Start what you do start — Right. Or else begin all over again. You can fondle the eggs of a Python but you can't play with the Python. You can break the bad habit today, but if you wait until tomorrow the bad Habit will break you.

Do the Right thing over and over again.